The Path to Equity

The Path to Equity

Inclusion in the Kingdom of Liberal Arts

Bill Coplin

ROWMAN & LITTLEFIELD
Lanham • Boulder • New York • London

Published by Rowman & Littlefield
An imprint of The Rowman & Littlefield Publishing Group, Inc.
4501 Forbes Boulevard, Suite 200, Lanham, Maryland 20706
www.rowman.com

86-90 Paul Street, London EC2A 4NE, United Kingdom

Copyright © 2023 by Bill Coplin

All rights reserved. No part of this book may be reproduced in any form or by any electronic or mechanical means, including information storage and retrieval systems, without written permission from the publisher, except by a reviewer who may quote passages in a review.

British Library Cataloguing in Publication Information Available

Library of Congress Cataloging-in-Publication Data

Names: Coplin, William D., author.
Title: The path to equity : inclusion in the kingdom of liberal arts / Bill Coplin.
Description: Lanham : Rowman & Littlefield, [2023] | Includes bibliographical references. | Summary: "The goal of this book is to convince liberal arts educators that preparing students for life should be a higher priority than preparing them to enjoy learning for its own sake"—Provided by publisher.
Identifiers: LCCN 2023010000 (print) | LCCN 2023010001 (ebook) | ISBN 9781475871326 (cloth) | ISBN 9781475871333 (paperback) | ISBN 9781475871340 (epub)
Subjects: LCSH: Education, Humanistic. | College students—Social conditions. | Learning—Philosophy. | Life skills—Study and teaching (Higher)
Classification: LCC LC1011 .C684 2023 (print) | LCC LC1011 (ebook) | DDC 370.11/2—dc23/eng/20230405
LC record available at https://lccn.loc.gov/2023010000
LC ebook record available at https://lccn.loc.gov/2023010001

To my wife Vicki whose support and love helped me in so many ways.

Contents

Acknowledgments	ix
Introduction	xi
PART I: BAIT AND SWITCH	1
Chapter 1: Knowledge Over Know-How	3
Chapter 2: Flawed Evidence	7
Chapter 3: The Incredible Bait Machine	11
PART II: ELITISM REVEALED	17
Chapter 4: Benjamin Franklin Is a Petite Bourgeoisie	19
Chapter 5: Dale Carnegie Is Not College Material	23
Chapter 6: *The Student Prince* Warning	27
Chapter 7: The Hereditary Kingdom	31
Chapter 8: What's in a Name	35
Chapter 9: The Liberal Arts Religion	39
Chapter 10: "Dumbing Down" Is Dumb	45
PART III: UNDERGRADUATE VICTIMS	51
Chapter 11: Commoners Vote with Their Feet	53
Chapter 12: The Anxiety Machine	57
Chapter 13: Career Services to the Rescue	67
Chapter 14: Experience Credit Ambivalence	71

PART IV: SOCIETAL DAMAGE — 77

Chapter 15: K–12 Toxicity — 79

Chapter 16: Unskilled Citizens — 89

Chapter 17: Too Many Thinkers; Not Enough Doers — 97

Chapter 18: Equity Denied — 105

PART V: FOUNDATIONAL CHANGES FOR EQUITY AND INCLUSION — 113

Chapter 19: Change PhD Education — 115

Chapter 20: Reform Lower Division Coursework — 123

Chapter 21: Undergraduates As Responsible Citizens — 129

Epilogue — 135

Index — 137

Acknowledgments

This book is a culmination of my more than 65 years of experience in higher education and my 60 years teaching college students. Faculty, colleagues, and students need to be acknowledged, if not blamed for what appears in these pages.

In writing this book, the most important person is Valerie Goldstein who as a college sophomore provided not just copy-editing services but research and content ideas throughout the book. Her support of the general theme of the book was vital to her ability to assist me. Her attention to detail, procedures for making changes, and policing me throughout the process make this book much better than it would have been without her. Actually, there probably would be no book without her.

Three other undergraduates played an important role in the development of the book. Dara Drake, who I met by phone when she was in high school and whose passion for reforming education is unlimited, provided me with research and joined me in a caper to spread the use of undergraduate TAs throughout Syracuse University. She gave me her time to comment and shape my thinking about all of undergraduate education as well as this book. Jamie Mauricio, one of my mentees, provided me with insight from his experience entering as a Syracuse freshman from Mexico and the process of applying to colleges in the United States as an international student. Mary Skuthan, who is going into Teach For America and committed to educational reform, worked with me in developing ways to help students in the Syracuse City School District gain the professional skills they are not getting from traditional K–12 programs. She introduced me to the Social Emotional Learning (SEL) movement which is designed to enrich K–12 education and avoid the overindulgence of the Kingdom's educational principles by our educators.

Two important sources of ideas on the role of career services in the Kingdom were Heather Robertson who is an expert on careers services and Kristen Aust who works to help students be ready for a viable career path that makes sense to the students. They were a great help thinking through the role of career services in the Kingdom.

Martha Diede, who shares with me the need to change undergraduate education, was a constant source of ideas as well as many criticisms for my views expressed in this book.

Two very important sources of support and inspiration over the years that motivated me to continue my mission and to write this book were Chancellor Kent D. Syverud and Peter Wilcoxen. Both recognized my success with students as well as my drive to change undergraduate education and more importantly inspired me to keep on my path. They sent me the message of "don't give up." Having two people who are dedicated so much to undergraduates telling me not to give up was crucial.

My agent Grace Freedson who has supported many of my projects read an initial proposal and said, "it might be tough to get it published, but I like it" and she found a publisher in a week. Thomas Koerner who represented Rowman & Littlefield was quick to accept and provided me constant feedback on how to try to not piss people off.

Finally, I want to mention one of my children, Laura, who allowed me almost every Sunday to ramble on about the book and guided me to alter the book from a negative muckraking rant to presenting a vision on how the Kingdom is already changing in the right direction and how it could speed up the process. When I followed her advice to not be so negative, I started to see that the Kingdom may be headed in the right direction and that the faculty of the Kingdom are good people.

Introduction

> Sow a thought, reap an action; sow an action, reap a habit; sow a habit, reap a character; sow a character, reap a destiny.
>
> —Steven Covey

The faculties of the Kingdom of Liberal Arts claim that living the life of the mind will enable undergraduates to have "lives of consequence, inquiry, and accomplishment," to use the subtitle of *The Evidence Liberal Arts Needs* published by MIT Press, by Richard A. Detweiler. Commoners might prefer becoming rich and famous or staying out of poverty.

Most of today's undergraduates are pursuing a college degree to have a satisfying economic future. But the Kingdom's business model of bait and switch promises career preparation and instead delivers scholarship of the various disciplines. The promises get undergraduates in the door under false pretenses. It is not something you would expect from those who say the best path to virtue and good citizenship is a liberal arts degree. A commoner might say faculties of liberal arts don't practice what they preach.

The term, "commoners," used throughout this book, is about undergraduates who think about college like petit bourgeoisie or peasants no matter what their socio-economic status is. They see education through the lens of a pragmatist who wants education to improve their chances of a happy life however they define it. To commoners, the college degree is a means to an end. The Kingdom's faculty, administrators, and supporters see education as an end in itself.

The majority of undergraduates since the GI Bill in 1945 are commoners under the rule of the Kingdom of Liberal Arts. Just like members of the medieval aristocracy who used their land to gain warriors as well as goods and services from their subjects, the promise of careers generates enrollment and therefore cash from today's college students. Land for servitude was a bad deal for vassals then just like the commoner's huge financial commitment for their BA or BS is a bad idea now. At different points of time and place, liberal arts undergraduates would be called peasants, serfs, slaves, sharecroppers, and vassals.

A medieval expert suggested that this metaphor is inappropriate because vassals will be killed if they don't work for the nobility while students have a choice to go to college. He has a point, but most students who go to liberal arts programs feel they have no choice. They go to college to have a solid economic foundation for a good life. They believe there is no other path.

This is not a knock against the life of the scholar whether it be in academia, the monastery, and some specialized area of study like the Talmud or Buddhism. People who choose a scholarly life should follow their interests. It is a knock against promising poorly informed students and their parents that the life of scholarship is a path to economic viability.

The Kingdom can save itself and once again prosper by following the principle of inclusion and treating undergraduates as if they were citizens in the Kingdom instead of commoners. The changes will be challenging for the faculty of the Kingdom. The changes are also challenging for undergraduates who need to see the faculty as trustworthy after decades of poor performance.

My hope is that this book will encourage liberal arts faculty to change their business model and provide an experience that prepares students for their careers and the goals they came to college to achieve. It is to convince the Kingdom that preparing students for life should be a higher priority than preparing them to enjoy learning for its own sake.

The book, perhaps naively, argues that as the faculty embraces a less parochial purpose for liberal arts education, the undergraduates will respond in a positive way. They will reduce some of their distrust of the Kingdom's faculty and administrators and join them, not as ignored and angry stakeholders, but as responsible citizens trusting faculty as the leaders they want them to be.

My views are formed by my personal experience at Syracuse University from over 50 years of teaching undergraduates and informed by defenders of liberal arts. Although SU may have many wealthy students and is a private research university, commoners are still in the majority. My many contacts with faculty and students from other institutions confirmed my view that the lack of trust between faculty and undergraduates resulting from the Kingdom's business model is similar to the liberal arts at other institutions.

Second, I have not focused on professional undergraduate programs. Because they require large numbers of liberal arts courses, much of my criticisms of the Kingdom apply to them. Many of their faculty are refugees from the Kingdom. Professional undergraduate programs were developed to avoid the bait and switch of liberal arts. They get a pass for this viewpoint despite exhibiting aristocratic tendency inherited from their mothership.

My credentials? I am a commoner who also is a member of the Kingdom of the Liberal Arts. I have worked to help commoners make sense out of college for more than 50 years through a major called Policy Studies located in a liberal arts program. I have worked with tens of thousands of students and have 2,000+ as advisees, many of whom I keep in touch with. My empathy for the confused and anxious undergraduate is based on my conversations with them as a teacher, advisor, and mentor.

I started my college journey when I was a 16-year-old freshman at Washington College on the promise of finding and preparing for a career path. I quickly discovered that the intended educational purpose of liberal arts colleges was to love the learning my professors loved. As a commoner, I was a victim of bait and switch.

After my freshman year, I transferred to Johns Hopkins where I earned my BA in Liberal Arts. I unknowingly jumped from the frying pan into the fire as a commoner would say. I made the switch because I did not like dorm life. I didn't even know Johns Hopkins was "ranked" way above Washington College in the minds of the aristocracy. This was before the ranking system racket was started by the *U.S. News and World Report* and reproduced by other publications. I had no idea that Johns Hopkins was the first university to embrace the German model of a research university which had spread across the United States. I was in the home of the devil and didn't even know it.

I did not know what I wanted to do after graduation but did know what I did not want: to become an academic, doctor, or lawyer like most Johns Hopkins liberal arts students. Participating in love of learning exercises captured my interest in many cases but was not my purpose. I was not aware of Career Services at Hopkins if there was even one in 1959. The only career advice I got was when my Spanish professor told me I should be a professor which made no sense to me because I was getting a B in his class.

Rejected by the Foreign Service at 20, I ended up first as a master's student and then a PhD student at the School of International Service, American University (AU). I pursued the Foreign Service and the graduate school because I found international relations interesting. I was a victim of a Liberal Arts myth that studying what interests you will help you decide on a career. This may work if you want to be an academic. It does not work for anybody else.

At AU while working on my degree, I taught on average two freshman courses each semester and received a PhD in four years. I realized that I wanted to be a college teacher. Looking back at that opportunity makes me think that the AU dean and some professors thought I was good at this scholarly stuff. They even sent me to be a teaching assistant for a professor at Howard University for three semesters.

I landed a tenure track position as an assistant professor at Wayne State University but left after the dean told me that I should maintain my impressive publication record rather than teach more freshman classes which I requested to do. After four years, I moved to Syracuse University in the College of the Arts and Sciences and the Maxwell School of Citizenship and Public Affairs.

I was a research wunderkind who published so much that I became a tenure full professor at the age of 39. I was also a teacher students wanted to be around thanks to my commoner roots and perspective.

I soon realized that a college teacher is not the same as a college professor. You could teach, but you had to publish in one or more academic fields. This was a form of bait and switch used to generate PhD recruits, which will be discussed further in Chapter 19.

I was a member of the Kingdom but never shared the mainstream scholarly goals of its faculty. I did not want to place research above teaching by ignoring the primary needs of undergraduates. I did not want to convince academically oriented students to become scholars.

I remain a commoner in the Kingdom who believed customers should receive what they pay for. My primary reference group became my students, not my faculty colleagues. My journey gives me a unique perspective to write this book about the dysfunction most commoners face as undergraduates and the difficult path to a better Liberal Arts Kingdom.

I am not advocating the end to liberal arts but a profound change in attitude and practice. The liberal arts faculties should do more for the commoners it seeks to serve. They should recognize that students are human beings who should be respected for their goals; not people to either become part of the Kingdom or dismissed with a diploma. Undecideds who go to college must have somewhere to go and for better or worse, Liberal Arts programs are their only choice.

The chapters are organized into five sections: (1) Bait and Switch, (2) Elitism Revealed, (3) Undergraduate Victims, (4) Societal Damage, and (5) Foundational Changes for Equity and Inclusion.

In each chapter of the first four sections, I have a section at the end of each chapter called "The Path to Equity and Inclusion" where I suggest what liberal arts faculty can better serve the commoners. The key to redemption is to establish a trustful relationship between faculty and students.

The first four Parts are written in the great tradition of muckraking for two reasons. First, this book follows a well-known tactic, "If you want to get a jackass's attention, hit him over the head with a two-by-four." Pointing out the similarities between today's liberal arts faculty and the nobility, crusaders, and other oppressors hopefully works like a two-by-four. Second, the muckraking orientation makes it a more interesting read where readers keep reading because they agree with the main point or are angered by it. It stirs up emotions, which are needed to change the faculty and undergraduate cultures that don't satisfy either.

Part V provides three more general changes that are necessary to create trust and collaboration between undergraduates and the faculty. The trust has been shattered by the Kingdom's bait and switch business model and by faculties' parochial over-commitment to the life of the mind.

The chapters are short. That is what commoners do. Longer chapters would give academic readers something to pick apart instead of getting the message that it is time for a change.

PART I

Bait and Switch

How the Kingdom of Liberal Arts' business model generates students but not career and citizenship readiness.

Chapter 1

Knowledge Over Know-How

> Education should turn out the pupil with something he knows well and something he can do well.
>
> —Alfred North Whitehead, *The Aims of Education*

Universities brand themselves as creators and transmitters of knowledge rather than providers of know-how. Knowledge has high status, especially for the Kingdom because of quotes like Isaac Newton's statement, "Knowledge is Power." "Knowledge" has high status in a world where the application of knowledge has brought great improvement in many aspects of life. The application is called know-how but for reasons to be discussed in later chapters, the Kingdom prefers knowledge over know-how as its brand.

Know-how is what undergraduates want, not knowledge for its own sake. Most commoners go to college seeking know-how because they assume it will lead to career success. The brand of knowledge is owned by the Kingdom of Liberal Arts and is considered a more prestigious label than know-how. Know-how is what plumbers do; knowledge is what the Kingdom does. The members of the Kingdom think they are better than the rest of the university because they value theory over application.

The Kingdom would not like to change from knowledge to know-how for two reasons. First, liberal arts defenders make a clear distinction between knowledge and vocational because they find career preparation as a goal distasteful and beneath them. They do not even like the more high-class version of vocational, "professional."

Second, the defenders think, probably correctly, that knowledge appeals to commoners more than know-how because most commoners want to be in the elite anyway even though they are not clear on what it means. The high cost of college tuition makes them want to get something special. Most commoners take a year or more of college to see they want know-how.

The Kingdom's antipathy to know-how is about both self-image and marketing. The more significant factor behind this antipathy is the faculty's self-image that knowledge creation and transmission is a higher-class activity than know-how. They also do not concern themselves with marketing. They want students to attend, but they see that as the job of admissions. They don't want to give up the ownership of the knowledge brand.

However, while the Kingdom says it is about knowledge, its faculty try to accommodate the desire for know-how among its customers. The Kingdom has started to talk about skills, rephrased by the aristocracy to a longer word "competencies" in their rhetoric. Pressure from outside the university has been leading to some willingness to see part of the mission as know-how but not to the degree that is required to build a solid relationship with undergraduates.

The skills offered by the Kingdom are not always the skills needed to succeed in careers other than in scholarship. To illustrate, the goals of most writing programs are to help students write in other courses, that is, write for various academic disciplines. There may be a course on general professional writing, but not offered at the lower division level. As anyone who reads professors' writing knows, writing to communicate to a wide variety of audiences is different from writing to other scholars.

To put it simply, the liberal arts does give academic credit for know-how, but it is the know-how of the professional scholar. The know-how is how to make proper academic citations, how to use the statistical tools used most by academics rather than in non-academic careers, how to conduct lab experiments, how to test hypotheses, how to perform literary criticism, and how to write an honors thesis. It's know-how for scholarly success rather than success outside of academia.

The Kingdom claims it is not a professional undergraduate program. But it is one, albeit to a very narrow audience of future professional scholars. If liberal arts programs were more explicit about its true mission, it would lose even more students than it does to the professional schools. As a result, most commoners are prevented from seeing the bias towards academic careers.

This discussion of know-how versus knowledge raises the obvious question about the conflict between the professional schools and the liberal arts college in universities. The former does know-how, like how to create a balance sheet in accounting, and the latter does knowledge for its own sake. If parts of universities do know-how and other parts do knowledge, why is only knowledge mentioned as the university's mission? The reason is that gaining knowledge is viewed as a higher level of learning. Professional school faculty tend to agree and much of the research they do is more knowledge than know-how. They have yet to free themselves from their mothership because most of them seek the approval of liberal arts faculty.

The use of knowledge as a brand by the Kingdom brings with it a downside that becomes more pronounced with each passing year. Given the high cost of tuition, and the disappointment that many parents have had themselves with their academic experience in college, the percentage of students choosing a professional undergraduate program has increased at the cost of enrollment in arts and science programs.

Yet the Kingdom sticks with the knowledge brand for much the same reason that blacksmiths stayed in the horseshoeing profession. It is something they have always done. With the commoner's confusion on the distinction between knowledge and know-how, the faculty can delude themselves that knowledge is preferred.

THE PATH TO EQUITY AND INCLUSION

The Kingdom needs to balance know-how and knowledge in their messaging. The balance would enhance recruiting and create a better framework for faculty and undergraduates to trust each other. It would better prepare students to think about their major and course choices when they begin college. It would send a signal to undergraduates that they are receiving what they are paying for and reduces some of the anxiety and hostility undergraduates now have toward the Kingdom and its faculty.

To make the messaging genuine, the Kingdom must add academic required courses that develop general professional skills that generate academic credit. Six credit hours would probably be enough as long as students could earn more credits through internships and other formal classes as electives.

The Kingdom has begun to do cosmetics by talking about careers and placement records in their advertising and putting a few more dollars into career services and other things outside of academics. They use terms like competencies and even skills and provide testimonials that illustrate career achievement.

Changing the messaging to give a bigger place to know-how could eventually promote change within the Kingdom. As the Kingdom works with strategic planning and forms of evaluations, its mission might eventually change. It would be one small step in the right direction of helping the Kingdom provide the know-how the students think they are paying for.

Chapter 2

Flawed Evidence

To generalize is to be an idiot.

—William Blake

The Kingdom presents three kinds of information to convince commoners that college is good for them. They are testimonials from successful people, systematic research, and the use of rankings. All three are seriously flawed, but they sell the bait.

Testimonials from alumni work just like they do for any sales pitch. What could be more powerful than statements by satisfied customers of the Kingdom? The more famous the celebrity, the more powerful the bait. Not only do the potential customers accept the credibility of the famed person, but they see the person as a role model. Michael Jordan sells sneakers and stimulates dreams of achievement; the Kingdom's rich and famous alums sell the college with the same results.

The trouble with the testimonial approach is that it uses what researchers call a one-shot case study, a deeply flawed research design. The shot is liberal arts, and the case is what alumni say about their liberal arts degrees. Testimonials are presented from those who think they did well and believe that the liberal education was a major contributing factor. With no control group and a small sample size, it is anecdotal. Students and parents know it is a flawed sample but do not care.

Alums who are not celebrities can be more important than the celebrities because there are more of them, and they can get right into the face of the potential customer. The colleges are pleased to connect their potential customers to vetted alums. The alums themselves are motivated to make the sale regardless of how the person they are talking to would fit. They may be participating in some type of competition with rivals of their alma mater. What alums would not like to report to friends that they convinced a student to go to their school instead of Harvard? Alums have tribal loyalty to their college because it was their rite of passage and not necessarily because it worked for them career-wise or they benefited from the academics.

A lot of people, including famous people, question these testimonials. If you search "successful people who never went to college" or "famous people who dropped out of college," you will find many articles that poke a hole in the Kingdom's messaging.

The second type of evidence that colleges provide is the use of systematic research. The research sometimes meets the standards of good social science research. It starts with large samples of people who may or may not be liberal arts degree holders. Some of these studies are conducted by proponents of the Kingdom even if they claim objectivity.

If we turn to the published research on the benefits and costs of the liberal arts, the message is not so clear even if the researchers are proponents of the liberal arts.

Two recently published books show how limited research supporting speculation about the consequences of liberal arts can be. (1) Richard A. Detweiler, *The Evidence Liberal Arts Needs: Lives of Consequences, Inquiry and Accomplishment,* and (2) Wendy Fischman and Howard Gardner, *The Real World of College: What Higher Education is and What it Can Be.* The former focuses only on liberal arts while the latter is more inclusive but tilts to the goals of liberal arts.

Both books say they are based on more than 1,000 interviews and are clearly well done by current standards of social science research. Their findings are as well documented as possible. Readers can make their own judgment on how much they want to trust the authors' findings.

The limitations of both books are substantial. The sample selection raises questions about whether the target population, to which they generalize their findings, is specifically liberal arts or just college graduates.

More importantly, the questions are based on viewpoints beyond "did your education prepare you for a career after college?" Instead of focusing on the heart of the bait and switch business model, they also ask the other questions. They posit elitist goals like leadership and the subtitle of the Detweiler book—"lives of consequences, inquiry and accomplishments." This assumes that the Kingdom's goals are what the students and their parents want.

The Fischmann/Gardner book reports that it asked undergraduates to rank the following four options of why they decided to go to college at the end of each interview:

To get a job
To gain different perspectives of people, knowledge, and the world
To learn to live independently

To study a particular content area in depth[1]

This list leaves out having fun and making my family happy, but to their credit, at least it lists jobs.

Many other factors can shape the opinions of their respondents so the causal link between the academic credit bearing experience and the attitudes of the responses cannot be demonstrated convincingly. The studies are much broader than focusing on career preparation, and they seek goals that are not the major interest of commoners.

Moreover, the findings on the outcome of a liberal arts education are mixed. The correlations and patterns are not impressive as they are in almost all educational research findings. Business leaders would not allow such tentative findings to guide their decision-making. Students and parents have no choice but to follow the PR around the studies unless they have the time to study the findings, which at a minimum would take hundreds of hours.

The Kingdom promotes the phrase "research based" to promote confidence in what is said. Very few readers or listeners will ask for citations and then look at the actual research. If they did, they would find the research is not as convincing as implied by the reflex phrase.

In addition, academic organizations like the American Association of Colleges and Universities (AAC&U) provide platforms for the distribution of research information. It promotes academic research and discussion to provide a cover for the Kingdom's sales pitch and the lack of convincing evidence.

A third type of evidence that could sell the value of college are the rankings ranging from *U.S. News and World Report* to studies published by research institutions on such topics of "Return on Investment." College PR machines will tout the findings if their institutions rank high. Because of the technical and complex ways these rankings are generated in addition to the fact that much of the data is reported by the colleges, the results are too general to ask the question whether or not the college is a good fit for any individual student.

Nonetheless, systematic research on the outcomes of liberal arts programs increases the beliefs of parents and students on the value of the program. They do so because the findings are simplified and summarized in the media and on book jackets. Reporters, who tend to buy the Kingdom's message anyway because they graduated in most cases from the Kingdom, repeat the research findings in their simplistic and watered-down style. The research is not as convincing and powerful as testimonials by famous and non-famous alums, but it is still part of the culture that cherishes the liberal arts.

The jury is out for whether or not liberal arts programs do or do not deliver their promise of career preparation. My own experiences and my work with undergraduates over 50 years is my main guide re-enforced by research by others. Social media and publications frequently raise questions about the usefulness of a liberal arts education. "Who Needs College" published in 1976 and "The War on College" published in 2018 are two *Newsweek* cover stories 42 years apart declaring that college has not worked for many.

The point is that the testimonials and professional research boosts the bait, and there is not much that can be done to neutralize it. Citing the many famous and successful people who question the testimonials that we mentioned before will not help. This will only lead to argumentative exchanges. Taking on the research establishment would be even more useless.

THE PATH TO EQUITY AND INCLUSION

Over the past decade, colleges conduct research on what percentage of students get jobs and what average salaries are after graduation. The difficulty in obtaining the data for all graduates raises questions about the findings. However, such records are valuable because they show that the Kingdom recognizes the responsibility for career development.

The Kingdom will keep using testimonials, systematic research, and references to rankings in its recruiting of undergraduates. If it wanted to build trust with its undergraduates, the colleges should add a statement on their marketing materials that "the past achievements of our graduates is no guarantee of the achievement of our future graduates."

Not only would that kind of phrasing be more truthful, but it would also send the message that all faculty and administrators would like to make clear to incoming students. "We provide you with opportunities to develop a bright future, but you must take advantage of those opportunities." This statement would promote a healthier relationship between undergraduates and the faculty because it would emphasize mutual responsibility.

NOTE

1. Wendy Fischman and Howard Gardner (2022), *The Real World of College: What Higher Education is and What it Can Be.* The MIT Press.

Chapter 3

The Incredible Bait Machine

> Man is the only kind of varmint [that] sets his own trap, baits it, then steps in it.
>
> —John Steinbeck

"College for all" is a pervasive and powerful attitude for most Americans. The forces supporting this attitude are overwhelming even as social and economic conditions provide more opportunities for non-college graduates through credentialing programs like coding. While this chapter focuses on college in general, the Kingdom especially benefits in attracting commoners perhaps because they are more frequently undecided and end up in liberal arts programs.

The appeal of college for all is based on fear and greed like most behavior. The fear factor is the risk of poverty and, more importantly, the stigma of not being a college graduate. Greed is self-interest making more money and having a higher self-perceived status. The bait machine plays on fear and greed so that most students are driven to a college no matter what their interests or talents.

THE K–12 EDUCATION SYSTEM

The bait is set early with the public and private K–12 schools where most of the curriculum is liberal arts prep. Those students who are viewed as college material receive most of the resources and most of the praise. Business tracks in high school and vocational programs are viewed by the majority of administrators, teachers, and guidance counselors as second class. Parents and students are socialized to follow the "college for all" mantra.

The non-college path as second class is a twisted version of the American Dream. Americans are driven to be winners which initially was defined as income. Horatio Alger wrote rags to riches novels aimed at motivating the poor to move out of poverty. The novels generated a concrete picture of the American Dream that took on mythical powers. The twist came when social status rather than money became the goal of the American dreamers. Graduating college became the path to not only money but to become an "educated person."

Including opportunities for students to develop their career skills in the K–12 curriculum has always been a theme, but never received enough support to bring it to the place it should be in the curriculum. In recent years, that pressure has increased from politicians, administrators, and parents to be more career focused.

However, the forces against change are powerful. Many professors do not want to change. The Kingdom's agents or more accurately lobbyists in the disciplinary high school fields like mathematics, English, and social studies keep adding latest content to be put in the curriculum. These agents lobby the state educational bureaucracies. Those with liberal arts elitist attitudes are more powerful than those who support applied skills and career exploration.

THE COLLEGE BOARD

This billion-dollar, self-funding non-profit puts the Kingdom's bait on steroids. The CEO David Coleman makes $2 million per year[1] and College Board had over $1 billion dollars in revenue in 2021.[2] They use this money to promote the Kingdom, which in turn, gets them more money.

They present studies that show a college is good for undergraduates and society. More important is offering AP credit for mostly liberal arts courses. Many universities and community colleges offer college credit in high school under the title concurrent enrollment. Add to that, the International Baccalaureate Program which is a higher-class form of liberal arts.

For the commoner as well as the rest of the students, these high school college credit options save money. For the more sophisticated students, the credits get them out of taking liberal arts courses in college. The appeal is overwhelming while it helps to trap students into liberal arts degrees.

The real consequences of the high school college credit are to get students convinced that they should go to college. Because most of the credits initially were from the Kingdom, it over-sells liberal arts courses. This is changing somewhat as professional schools accept the liberal arts credits and are generating some college credit courses in their fields.

The College Board and related activities like the SATs start forcing students and parents to invest in going to college as early as the 9th or 10th grade. Once the down payment is made, they tend to want to continue this path because they "do not want to waste the money they have already sunk into the enterprise."

COLLEGE RANKINGS

U.S. News and World Report created a big business out of college rankings. Other publications have done the same. College administrators take rankings very seriously because they believe they generate sales. If they have high rankings, they advertise them. If the colleges have low rankings, they complain and take action to make their rankings look better.

Meanwhile, the commoners pay attention. They believe that the higher the ranking, the more likely they will be in a better career path when they graduate. Their families and friends are eager to congratulate or criticize. The high schools brag about their students who gain acceptance at high-ranking colleges. This creates competition among students, families, and schools that contribute to focusing on the wrong question.

Instead of asking which college is a better fit or should they go to college, they focus on which is the highest ranked college to get into. They assume the higher the rank the better education they will get and the higher they will go in life.

The rankings tend to be based on research output and dollars generated for research as hard data mixed in with some student surveys and measures. The rating systems claim to balance research and teaching, but research seems to play a larger role than it deserves if the question is which college will help a student find a satisfying career.

Most students realize that the reason higher ranked schools are better at career opportunities is because they provide better networks than the lower ranked schools rather than the quality of their educational programs. They may be correct.

Regardless of the usefulness of college rankings, the overall effect seems to be increasing the attractiveness of the bait. Given the other powerful forces pushing for liberal arts and college in general, the rankings have the effect of increasing the college going rate. It creates competition that motivates students to apply to college because they want to "win" the admission to a top-ranked school. Also, they don't really have a good idea of what they want to get out of college so why not try for the highest rank?

THE UNITED STATES MILITARY

When one thinks of the role the armed forces played in generating college students, the GI Bill is usually considered. However, the GI Bill in 1946 was only the beginning. The federal government has been pumping money into programs ever since. With the ending of the draft in the 1970s the incentives to attract volunteers have grown tremendously.

However, while the initial GI bill generated applicants to liberal arts programs, the support of the education of veterans has increasingly generated students who have chosen professional undergraduate programs over liberal arts programs. Veterans are likely to be commoners, so this pattern reflects their perceptions that liberal arts programs will not serve their economic needs. See Chapter 14 for more on the decline in liberal arts enrollments.

ADMISSIONS SPENDING

Colleges and universities play a big role increasing the college going rate. They are in a competition race with each other so like all business, marketing is increased. Large amounts of money are spent by colleges to attract applicants. The overall result of this is market saturation that convinces students and parents that college is a necessity.

Admissions people always approach the high school student assuming the student plans to go to some college. Maybe some students might say "I'm not sure I want to go to college," but most will not. If they are thinking about not going to college, the interaction with admissions people, juiced up by guidance counselors and peers, will end that thought. If the student is not interested in a professional program, the admission person will suggest the courses of the Kingdom. If the student is not strong enough to get into a professional school, the recommendation will be to join the Kingdom's program and transfer to the professional program next year.

THE PATH TO EQUITY AND INCLUSION

The college bait machine is not likely to weaken but more likely to increase over time. To create the basis in high school that will lead to a more trusting relationship in college between faculty and undergraduates, two things have to happen.

The first is that the K–12 system must reduce the focus and rewards of college preparation in their program. Guidance counselors must convince students and parents that the selection of a college should be based on the fit between the students and the college. Leaders of the K–12 education system must see their mission as helping students make good decisions about what they will do after high school. Some progress has been made with increased vocational education and acquiring skills needed for the workforce, but the pressures from the lobby groups and teachers on school administrators create a barrier to the change. Resources are needed to provide some space for students to think about alternatives which is not likely to be enough. A small start would be to bring alums from all walks of life into the elementary schools to help students understand the options early in their life.

Guidance counselors have little desire or capacity to inform their students of alternatives to college. They are hesitant to advocate alternatives because they may anger parents, disappoint students, and face criticism from the school's leadership. In addition, guidance counselors can have as many as 400 students to advise which would not allow them to get into heavy duty discussions with students who should be weighing alternatives.

The second powerful change would be for universities to increase the seats for professional undergraduate programs. Large numbers of commoners might want to get into a professional program at a state or private university but are denied because there is not enough capacity. This means that undergraduates are entering college in a program they do not want to be in. What could be worse in damaging the trust between undergraduates and faculty from the first day in college?

NOTES

1. Matt Eck. "The College Board Profits off Students' Anxieties about College Admissions." *Daily Trojan*, 16 Sept. 2021, https://dailytrojan.com/2021/09/16/the-college-board-profits-off-students-anxieties-about-college-admissions/.

2. *Follow the Money—College Board Finances*. https://www.totalregistration.net/AP-Exam-Registration-Service/Follow-The-Money-History-of-College-Board-Finances.php. Accessed 28 Jan. 2023.

PART II

Elitism Revealed

How and why elitism reigns in the Kingdom.

Chapter 4

Benjamin Franklin Is a Petite Bourgeoisie

> I need anything, anything that will stop me from living in the kind of death the bourgeois eat, the death called comfort.
>
> —Kathy Acker

I published an article in the *Chronicle of Higher Education* in 2004, "Lost in the Life of the Mind," describing my surprise and disappointment at the bait and switch model that victimized me when I was a college freshman. The article generated comments like a professor telling me to take "one more course in political science, and this time pay attention" or another professor saying, "Coplin's ostensible message is stubborn philistinism that has been around since the earliest days of the American republic." Could a philistine be a commoner? He went on to say that the Coplins of our culture would prefer *American Idol* or *Survivor* over reading Nabokov. If he cared about students, maybe he would have conducted a survey among commoners of their preference for Nabokov over some current TV show. Or maybe he would not like the results.

I responded to this display of elitism with Shakespeare.

"To paraphrase the Bard, hath not a philistine a brain and a soul? If you prick us, are we not conscious of what has happened? If we read or see something we find distasteful, will we not be as appalled as some are by *American Idol* and *Survivor*? If we value money, will we not help others?"

These reactions to the article are examples of the parochialism of the Kingdom's faculty which can be stated as "what I liked learning, my students must like learning." Projecting one's own likes and dislikes on others is a violation of the principle of a liberal approach to education. It's okay to think that because I like Nabokov, my students should be given the opportunity to like Nabokov. It is not okay to make a requirement around Nabokov leading to a grade which leads to graduation if inclusion is the goal.

An English professor dismissed the article as old fashioned culture war stuff. I corresponded with this learned aristocrat through email. After a few exchanges, he asked me in frustration who I thought represented the highest intellectual level. Unaware of the imminent doom that was to follow, I responded "Benjamin Franklin." He told me Franklin was a petit bourgeois, which I presume is one of the worst things a scholar can be called.

The professor's hostility was most likely based on Franklin's popular book, *Poor Richard's Almanac*. Aside from being a commercial success, something the Kingdom finds distasteful, the book was a self-help book (more about that in the next chapter) and was full of useful quotes from various historical figures. It is a book helping commoners get the value of historical scholars and others who, according to Franklin, said something useful.

The English professor's dismissiveness of Franklin touches on something that Franklin was worried about. He did not want American higher education to be a repeat of the aristocratic nature of European education.

Franklin created an academy in Pennsylvania, which was the start of the University of Pennsylvania, to educate American youth, quite radical for the time because most American elites would send their children to European universities. He proposed experience-based, practical curricula. For example, he incorporated gardening in the curriculum—an effective way to teach science that is both understandable and useful. Unfortunately, later leaders of Penn and existing American academics did not share his view that the useful was more important than, as Franklin called it, the "ornamental."

His disdain for elitist institutions is apparent in his view of Harvard. He wrote "Harvard students learn little more than how to carry themselves handsomely and enter a room genteelly (which might as well be acquired at dancing school) and from whence they return, after an abundance of trouble and charge, as great blockheads as ever, only more proud, and self-conceited."[1] He liked to quote Native Americans who told him that when they sent their children to colleges, they learned nothing useful.

Benjamin Franklin was born a commoner who approached everything in the spirit of problem-solving to meet his needs and the needs of society. He saw the value of collective problem-solving and incorporated it into many of his accomplishments. He invented, founded, and discovered:

- The lightning rod
- Bifocals
- The Franklin stove
- The Library Company of Philadelphia (America's first circulating library)
- Union Fire Company (America's first volunteer fire department)

- American Philosophical Society (America's first learned society)
- Pennsylvania Hospital (America's first public hospital)
- The Philadelphia Contributionship (America's first mutual insurance company)
- That lead caused sickness
- That the common cold spread between people in indoor air[2]

The professor's refusal to see Franklin as an intellectual is strange given Franklin's mastery and contribution to science at the time or his creativity in coming up with ideas that solved problems. It reflects a general viewpoint discussed in chapter 1 that knowledge is superior to know-how.

Not that Franklin couldn't play the role of aristocrat which he did in Paris as an ambassador of the colonies. He was a favorite of the upper crust and had a lot of fun. But he never took that or himself too seriously.

The English professor is right, Franklin is a petite bourgeoisie. What is so bad about that?

THE PATH TO EQUITY AND INCLUSION

To move the liberal arts curriculum to engage commoners, the Kingdom needs to have space for doers who are also thinkers. The preference for knowledge over know-how needs to be reduced so that every course enables students to see how problems were solved and the practical consequences of scholarly theories.

The introductory study of chemistry should not just be about Chemistry as a science but also about the methods in the physical sciences and how chemistry has led to improvements in medicine, the environment, and production of goods and services. Humanity courses should not just be about the scholarship of the fiction and non-fiction writers but also how the courses can help students think about their own lives. Social Science courses should not just present theories of the specific field but also teach the limitations of social science methods and how the public, private, and nonprofit sectors can help reduce societal problems.

How much of these suggestions should be covered in these courses is up to the teachers or the departments, but it should be between 20% and 50% of course content. The bourgeoisie would appreciate that as would all commoners. Elite students who aspire to be in the Kingdom would also like it unless they want to be scholars and find it too mundane.

NOTES

1. *Founders Online: Silence Dogood,* No. 4, 14 May 1722. University of Virginia Press, http://founders.archives.gov/documents/Franklin/01-01-02-0011. Accessed 28 Jan. 2023.

2. "Fact Sheet: Benjamin Franklin's Inventions." *Visit Philadelphia,* https://www.visitphilly.com/media-center/press-releases/fact-sheet-benjamin-franklin-inventions/. Accessed 28 Jan. 2023.

Chapter 5

Dale Carnegie Is Not College Material

Education is the ability to meet life's situations.

—John G. Hibben, former president of Princeton University

In 2015, I proposed adding Dale Carnegie's book, *How to Win Friends and Influence People,* to one of my classes at Syracuse University, and an associate dean from the College of Arts and Sciences told me not to because most faculty did not consider Dale as college material. I included Carnegie in the course regardless.

Dale Carnegie wrote one of the most-used books of the twentieth century. Translated into more than 31 languages, *How to Win Friends and Influence People* is the eighth-most-read book in the NYC Public Library system and the only nonfiction book in the top ten,[1] and a 2013 Library of Congress survey ranked Carnegie's volume as the seventh most influential book in American history.[2] If countless adults who patronize the public library of New York City read Dale Carnegie, undergraduates from all walks of life should too.

The title *How to Win Friends and Influence People* only hints at what the book offers. It is not just about sales but is also about all facets of people skills. It helps people from all backgrounds learn about working constructively with and learning from others, career exploration and success, and fostering collective and community problem-solving.

It is too bad most academics don't see it that way. To that administrator and many others in the academic culture, "not college material" is used to mean too simple. Carnegie did to the field of psychology what McDonald's did to hamburgers—he took the theories of great scholars like Plato and Socrates and made those ideas simple and accessible to everyone. Like Franklin, he wanted to communicate the great ideas he had to the people in terms they could understand.

The number one goal of self-help writers is to write so that all readers can understand what they are saying and to gain know-how. Clarity and usefulness to the commoners is not the number one goal of academic researchers. Their number one goal is to provide knowledge that reflects the scholarly theories of their colleagues as well as to provide detail that they think elaborates their theories, but commoners have trouble understanding.

The contrast is particularly relevant to the teaching of psychology in the Kingdom. Because students are concerned about how to get along with people in their daily lives whether it is in their family, among their peers, or dealing with people in authority, they will take introduction to psychology courses thinking that is the know-how they will get. They don't understand that the psychology courses are about the "scientific" field of psychology, that is what professors in the field talk to each other about. Many psychology professors link the field to application in their lectures, but more do not.

This is why works like Dale Carnegie's have never been included in undergraduate education. Carnegie's works are in the self-help genre, which academics don't like. Self-help books place know-how above knowledge, practice above theory, and action above speculation. Most college professors prefer the reverse. Self-help books help readers become what they want to be rather than what the professors want them to think. Self-help books provide what most undergraduates thought they were going to get from a college degree.

Dale Carnegie approached Columbia University to hire him to teach a course based on his ideas. Columbia rejected him. He was a commoner not welcomed in the Kingdom. He approached the YMCA in New York City which served the rich and the poor to give lectures on his book. His lectures were standing room only and his book gave him the resources to educate millions of people around the world.

Columbia University not only lost a profit center but helped set a pattern of learning outside of academia. Today, the websites have placed academic institutions in a vulnerable position because commoners have found a workaround. This is especially true for self-help books. The treatment of Dale Carnegie and also Benjamin Franklin shows the tension between knowledge, the preferred idiom of the Kingdom, and know-how, what commoners really want.

If Carnegie were alive today, he would see the web as another source of education for all people and be pleased. Steve Watt's biography of Carnegie describes Carnegie's view in the 1940s that "standard course offerings in American high school and colleges were archaic . . . 'medieval,' 'silly, ineffectual and benighted.'"[3] He saw the Liberal Arts Kingdom for what it was: scholasticism and not know-how.

Most liberal arts faculty would never accept that Dale Carnegie and other self-help manuals should be part of the college curriculum because it would be viewed as "training." Apparently, training is too low class for the life of the mind because it is not "education." Better to read psychological theories because it is education than to develop people skills because it is training!

But wait a minute, don't liberal arts faculty train on citation requirements, and methods in the sciences and social sciences? Don't they use their classes to train students to think like them whether it is America is a great country or America is a rotten country? The difference between training and education is not as clear as the Kingdom would have us think.

Is education an activity where the learning outcome is too general to be observed while training has more specific learning outcomes? Is education an activity in the life of the mind and is training an activity where students change their behavior? Is education an end in itself, and training a means to an end?

Dale Carnegie was a problem solver who wrote self-help books. His two main books were on two different problems he saw people needed help with. *How to Win Friends and Influence People* helps people to get along with others, not just for business but for everything in life. The other less well-known book was written after World War II. *How to Stop Worrying and Start Living: A Handbook on Conquering Work and Fears* was written because he felt anxiety was rampant in America.

Fear and anxiety continue to grow, particularly among undergraduates. The discussion of mental health in college education today is increasing and so is evidence of the concern Dale Carnegie expressed in the 1940s and 1950s. Instead of helping our undergraduates deal with these concerns in credit-bearing classes, the Kingdom prefers the job be done in non-credit bearing experiences where those who perhaps needed it most are likely to avoid the voluntary opportunity until they cannot function anymore.

Too bad the Kingdom doesn't allow self-help books in its undergraduate curriculum. Too bad the life of the mind does not include know-how. Too bad the needs of commoners are ignored.

THE PATH TO EQUITY AND INCLUSION

The point of this chapter is not that practicing Dale Carnegie should be in every college, but that self-help manuals should be used especially in lower division courses. The popularity of the books should not be a barrier to their use in undergraduate education. These and many other self-help manuals need to have large audiences of commoners. If they do, more students will become engaged. They will stop asking "Why am I studying this?" because they will be able to immediately apply things to their life. These books are accessible to all students rather than the few who love learning for its own sake.

The relevance question is a source of distrust between undergraduates and faculty. It sounds to undergraduates too much like parents saying eat your spinach. Many topics taught by the Kingdom's faculty appear to be irrelevant to the lives of undergraduates. Faculty have difficulty explaining why subjects are relevant except to say, "it is good for you," but that does not help build trust.

NOTES

1. *Top 10 Checkouts of All Time | The New York Public Library*. https://www.nypl.org/125/topcheckouts. Accessed 28 Jan. 2023.

2. Steve Watts (2013), *Self-Help Messiah: Dale Carnegie and Success in Modern America*. Other Press.

3. Watts, *Self-Help Messiah*.

Chapter 6

The Student Prince Warning

> The main value of college is providing discipline by completing annoying homework assignments and hanging around with people of the same age before entering the workforce.
>
> —Elon Musk

Since its inception, most students have never found undergraduate education of much use. The operetta, movie, and Broadway show called *The Student Prince* makes this point very clear. It had a broad following in America from the 1920s to the 1950s. Google *The Student Prince* or watch it on Netflix if you want to get a more detailed picture.

Here is a quick summary. The story is about an Austrian prince who was, like most teenagers, not ready for adulthood. He was sent to college by his parents to get straightened out. While there, he fell in love with a commoner barmaid that he met while drinking, of course. When his father, the king, looked like he might die, the prince was forced to go home. He dumped the barmaid and assumed the role his family planned for him.

The plot is not the point even though it is something millions of commoners found entertaining. It is like many novels and plays about the role of elitism in the relationship among lovers. Nor is it the point that the Student Prince was a pervasive cultural artifact in the 1920s through the 1950s in the entertainment industry, Broadway shows, and other things. The point is captured in the lyrics of one of the songs, Students March Song "Let's All be Gay Boys." Forget how that title fits in in 2022 and the sexist nature of the lyrics and the entire play. Instead, read some of the lyrics,

"Cato, Plato, Cicero, They all make me sickero! Homer, Xrxes, Xenophn, Twice as bad! All good teachers go to Hades! Chemistry Advanced Biology Do not merit an apology. Higher math stirs up wrath, Latin prose thumber your nose . . . history a mystery."[1]

Even in the good old days of the Kingdom, liberal arts never fit the needs of most students, even members of the aristocracy. A few of these students may have liked scholarly activities and perhaps behaved themselves. Evidence of this student dissatisfaction is demonstrated by the fact that undergraduates created trouble in the town with their violent and immature activities. Many towns refused to let college build near them; others saw it as a distasteful economic development option.

Today college students continue the tradition of making a lot of trouble on campus and in the surrounding areas. They engage in alcohol and drug abuse, racial discrimination, sexual harassment, and all kinds of disturbances. The job of the traditional residential college is to provide a rite of passage for its students, and the process is not always pretty. Because academics is not the main focus for the vast majority of students, they have more time and energy to cause trouble.

The long-term commercial success of *The Student Prince* may have been a result of the music, or the story, or values of the production, but I prefer to think it was that the commoners in the audience who had gone to college were happy to see liberal arts get its comeuppance.

THE PATH TO EQUITY AND INCLUSION

If liberal arts faculty were to appreciate the lesson here that liberal arts was born out of religion, captured in part by the physical sciences and then "aped" by the social sciences, they would understand the aristocratic nature of the content. They would understand why Franklin made the distinction between ornamental and useful. They would also understand that undergraduate education from its inception never appealed to the bulk of adolescents, even though most of them initially came from the elite. They would stop wishing for the good old days where liberal arts education was successful. There were no good old days for undergraduates except for those teenagers inclined to be scholars.

The lesson here is faculty and to a lesser extent administrators need to take a hard look at liberal arts education. They need to recognize how commoners feel about being forced to take distribution requirements. It never worked for the commoner in the past and present. It works even less today.

NOTE

1. *The Student Prince* (1954). Directed by Joe Pasternack, performances by Ann Blyth, Edmund Purdom, John Ericson, Louis Calhern, Edmund Gwenn, S. Z. Sakall, and Betta St. John, Metro-Goldwyn-Mayer.

Chapter 7

The Hereditary Kingdom

> A celibate clergy is an especially good idea, because it tends to suppress any hereditary propensity toward fanaticism.
>
> —Carl Sagan

Many faculty members in the Kingdom of Liberal Arts come from families who are or were also in the Kingdom. According to one study, "tenure-track faculty come from homes wealthier than the average population and are 25 times more likely than the general population to have a parent with a Ph.D."[1] They are also more likely to value learning for the sake of learning.

Some commoners like me, who made it into the Kingdom from a family with only a high school diploma or less, are not comfortable with the Kingdom's elitist proclivities. These commoners wanted to focus on teaching and not research. Many professors who came from the ranks of commoners have received awards for outstanding teaching but did not receive tenure because they did not spend enough time doing research. Chapter 19 discusses how PhD education has to change to allow more commoners into the ranks of professors.

The hereditary factor may be a result of genes or the environment the person grew up in. It doesn't really matter. The academic tribe is self-generating and loyal to the role of scholar above all else. There is no more proof of this than the extraordinary efforts with very poor results of recruiting people of color who are much more likely than others to not have family academic connections. Conversely, many of the students of color who get a PhD and become members of the Kingdom have family connections to academia.

In addition, the widespread practice of sanctioned nepotism where universities hire the partner of faculty members they want increases the percentage of those from academic families. Whether these partners are from academic families is not as important as the fact that both are in the same culture, re-enforcing the commitment to research and the tendency to look for students who are scholars.

Liberal arts faculty are from families where they have acquired ideas about education that fit the Kingdom's view of creating "educated" people. Whether this is done from a desire to "civilize" commoners or the desire to help their students have a better intellectual life, the faculty of the Kingdom want to make their students become more like them. They are missionaries for scholarship just as their forefathers were.

Even in this day where diversity, inclusion, and equity are so powerful in the culture of higher education, college public relations stories about how a professor is a third generation PhD seem to appear as frequently as stories about a professor who emerged from a life of poverty. Apparently, hereditary has some sales appeal in the recruiting wars. It certainly does to the members of the Kingdom.

People whose families were in the academic business have an advantage over commoners who may have a desire to join the Kingdom. They know much more about the academic business than commoners just like shoemakers know more about making shoes. Both tend to be family businesses.

Commoners don't start out knowing that being a professor is primarily about research. They think they will primarily be teachers and that their research output will not make or break them. This naivete encourages them to pursue the goal of becoming a college professor. Some commoners fortunately realize it by their junior year and are turned off. Many don't realize it until they are in graduate school and sometimes floundering. Many do not complete their PhDs and, if they do, have trouble getting tenure.

If the stock of liberal arts faculty come from families of other faculty, today's faculty may see their job as creating "educated" people just like them. Today, it's just scholars. The life of the mind will always be at the center of what their teaching is all about and why many of them cannot connect with their commoner students.

THE PATH TO EQUITY AND INCLUSION

The pattern of many faculty coming from the academic family business is not going to change. The only way to help promote reform is to help all students, regardless of their inherent love of learning. Faculty must find room in their hearts for the commoners.

The Kingdom's faculty must see how they need to balance their teaching to be about both the life of the mind and life. For many faculty, this will require a sea-change in the way they go about their teaching activities. Since change is difficult, individuals whose culture is shaped by the scholarly love of learning will face a traumatic choice between keeping their cultural heritage and helping all students prepare for life after college. If they are committed to equity and inclusion, they don't have to give up their cultural heritage. The just need to make some room in their approach and their degree requires that give more value to commoners.

NOTE

1. *Academia Is Often a Family Business. That's a Barrier for Increasing Diversity | Science | AAAS.* https://www.science.org/content/article/academia-often-family-business-s-barrier-increasing-diversity. Accessed 28 Jan. 2023.

Chapter 8

What's in a Name

> The name of a thing does not matter as much as the quality of the thing.
>
> —William Shakespeare, *Romeo and Juliet*

Undergraduates are not sure what to call their professors. Should it be "Dr." or "Professor" or their first name? The uncertainty is an indicator of the uneasy relationship between undergraduates and faculty members.

Ascribed educational authority is needed for children and adults although it varies at different ages. It only works for adults or wanna-be adults if the professor has a weapon, which in this case is the all-powerful grade. The authority of the professor is like the authority of a tyrant if trust is lacking. As stakeholders, fear rather than love or mutual respect motivates them. The club of grades might be required for first year students to open the possibility for eventual respect, but it is not a long-term solution. Reluctance to accept the authority of the faculty is evidence of the confusion undergraduates bring to their views of professors and much of their distasteful behavior toward the faculty.

Commoners can be heard saying that the term "PhD" means "piled higher and dryer." This characterization is what you would expect from those who resent the long sentences and new words created by PhDs and the use of grades, rather than relevance, to stimulate engagement.

Commoners have trouble with the idea that PhDs should be called "doctors" because they are not medical doctors saving lives. Medical doctors have a goal which is to promote health, something the commoner can understand. Commoners are not sure what the PhD's goal of scholarship means but are sure that it does not deserve the same status as a medical doctor.

Commoners are confused because the PhD is a Doctor of Philosophy rather than Doctor of what they actually got their degree in. Why is it not Doctor of Economics for Economists for example?

People outside of academia have trouble with the terms professor, Doctor, and PhD. A CEO for a company in which a colleague and I worked running a profit center would refer to us as the professors. Because of his stated hostility to Harvard where he received some kind of degree or training, we knew he was making fun of us. He listened to us because we brought his firm recognition and money, but he just couldn't resist sticking it to us.

Think about how the word "academic" is used outside of academia and even by academics themselves. The phrase "it's academic" frequently means that it is theoretical and not important. It's a title for TV shows and contests in high school or college which indicates that it is a form of game playing. However, when it comes to college credit, the credit must be "academic." The confusion over the meaning of academic reflects a broader confusion over the proper role of professors.

The term "professor" makes sense to the Kingdom's faculty members because they see themselves primarily as scholars which by implication means their value is in transmitting their scholarship. Commoners who came to college to get a better life have trouble figuring out how scholarship will lead to a better life. They might prefer the words "expert," "researcher," or "teacher." They don't understand that scholars are those who engage in exchanges among other scholars in their field to explore their ideas and raise their status. They don't get the difference between a researcher who is writing to present a viewpoint to people outside of academia and a researcher who is writing only to the other scholars in the field.

When I received my PhD, a mentor said to me "you are now a gentleman and a scholar." I was confused by this comment. What does a PhD have to do with being a gentleman? Today the term would be a "gentleperson." Maybe the mentor meant a scholar is a civilized human being. Many defenders of liberal arts say that scholarship will help students to understand what it means to be human. The life of the mind is assumed to be the primary source of humanizing.

I have students call me Coach Coplin or Coplin. I don't want them to call me Bill because I am not interested in friendship. I do not want them to call me professor because I don't see my job as "professing." My job is to help them succeed in developing their skills to have a career path they will be happy with and, for my field, to make sense of the policy-making process. My job is not to deposit stuff in their heads. That most professors would prefer to be called Professor or Dr. is indicative of the faculty's view that they are the authority, and the student is the receiver of the knowledge. A student told me that her professor said that if an email sent to him does not say "professor" or "doctor," he will delete it. This professor should not be criticized. He was enforcing the culture of the Kingdom.

"Professor" is a term most used by college students. In high school, those in authority were called teachers. In teaching them to ski, they were called instructors. In coaching the school's volleyball team, they were called coaches. The term "mentor" is like a coach and some, but too few, undergraduates see a faculty member as their mentor.

"Professor "or "Doctor" carries with it authority and implies respect. In college, this ascribed authority was needed because students have trouble understanding their professors and are rarely impressed by their personality, lecturing ability, or usefulness. The current generation of teenagers are stingy with their acceptance of authority anyway, so the faculty is faced with a challenge to their authority and find respect hard to come by.

THE PATH TO EQUITY AND INCLUSION

In order to promote equity and inclusion, the Kingdom needs to encourage undergraduates to accept a more cooperative relationship and see the faculty as their helpers in their quest for a good life. The term "professor" is not likely to wither away, but a view of what professors should do for students could change if the faculty could bring themselves to help students explore and develop not just their intellectual capacity, but their skills and life goals. This goal view is less radical than it may seem to be. It is similar to the idea of "mentor" which has long been viewed as an important role for the Kingdom's faculty.

The idea that faculty should be mentors to students is well accepted in the Kingdom. However, too many mentorships are to improve the scholarship of students, which in its more intensive form is what faculty do for their PhD students. As a result, the vast majority of undergraduates don't have faculty mentors in college because they are less enthusiastic about becoming a scholar than their faculty. Mentorships need to be available to all students and need to be broader than just improving scholarship.

For the Kingdom's faculty members to establish a useful and trusted relationship with undergraduates, they must provide whatever help they can to students in both their academic and career pursuits. They must resist the temptation to push their "best" students into academic professions and face the challenge of helping the bulk of undergraduates think about their career and life future. To be more specific, they must help students see the trade-offs between doing good and doing well. When they ask about students' interests, it should not just be what subject interests them, but what they like doing. Asking if students like working with people or data is one key question, for example.

Faculty members need to be mentors for life and not just the life of the mind. They need to help students think about how their whole college experience, not just their academic experience, will get them on a valuable path after they graduate. They don't need to tell their students what to do but ask questions to help students figure it out. They also need to help students realize that everything they do during their four years in college will impact where they are when they graduate. They need to emphasize the importance of general skills and that college is a gymnasium to practice and improve skills as well as explore career options.

This is a big ask for faculty because PhD training discussed in Chapter 19 and the importance of the scholarly way of life are what the Kingdom's faculty see as their job. They might oppose this requirement on the grounds that they lack training and knowledge to be a life mentor and don't have the time or inclination to study the job market. They need to remember that expertise and knowledge is not the biggest requirement for effective mentoring, but that the willingness to listen and withhold judgment is the primary requirement. Their job is to encourage their students' self-reflection and to play the role of a caring human being.

To be a basic life mentor for their students does not require faculties to give up their love and pursuit of scholarship. They can continue to be stimulated and enjoy that role as well as help the few students who share their passion move into that role. They just have to figure out a way to give all their students the skills, perspectives, and opportunities to find a profession other than scholar and to design liberal arts programs to prepare for life other than traditional scholarly activities. Ultimately, this means changing their priorities from scholar to coach or mentor of undergraduates.

Chapter 9

The Liberal Arts Religion

> At your highest moment, be careful, that's when the devil comes for you.
>
> —Denzel Washington

The members of the Kingdom believe that all things in the Kingdom lead to and from scholarship. The idea that study and reflection with other scholars will lead to better and happier college graduates is based on faith more than empirical evidence. The Kingdom's faculty members are true believers in the liberal arts religion.

The Kingdom's never-ending justifications are religious-like. They appear in countless books and articles defending liberal arts and through several associations of scholars. Two prominent associations are the National Association of Scholars (NAS), which advocates for old-fashioned liberal arts, and the American Association of Colleges & Universities (AAC&U), which uses as its byline on its website in September 2022 "A Voice and a Force for Liberal Education."[1] The AAC&U represents both the old fashioned and the reformists factions.

The Kingdom's classification of faculty as PhDs, Professors, and Doctors is similar to religious leaders' and teachers' titles of Minister, Iman, Priest, and Rabbi. The Kingdom's dedication to scholarship is similar to the monks who spend their time studying religious writing amongst themselves.

Monks live in poverty and spend all their time in scholarship activities while academic scholars use their scholarship to pursue a professional career. They entered PhD training to pursue scholarship, but they frequently need to teach undergraduates and take on other duties.

The Kingdom is driven by the sanctity of scholarship which leads to constant conflict with administrators who must worry about student satisfaction. The administrators at research universities especially, but also liberal arts colleges, believe they are required to embrace the sanctity of scholarship, or they will lose their "best and brightest" scholarly faculty. While the administrators are outspoken on the top priority of scholarship, they still have to remind members of the Kingdom that undergraduates pay their salaries. Some traditional faculty members find that off-putting.

One might draw a rough analogy with the current governance of Iran and Saudi Arabia. The governments of both countries are challenged by the religious scholars, who are holding on to the past. They resist the reality that governments need to adapt to changing world conditions by paying attention to their citizens. The faculty in the liberal arts Kingdom are inherently conservative when it comes to their relationship to undergraduates. They are more concerned with academic standards than they are with student success and see themselves as missionaries to bring the students into the fold. Moving toward a more productive role with undergraduates would threaten their core beliefs despite the obvious need to do so.

Like all religions, the Kingdom has a business plan. The business plan is to sustain and grow the commitment to scholarship as the supreme value through the bait and switch model. It is out of step to some degree with the mission of most universities. The ultimate test of a religion is the ability to recruit and satisfy its members. Given its reliance on the bait and switch model, the Kingdom is having a tough time with that task as suggested in Chapter 11, Commoners Vote with Their Feet.

The liberal arts religion is a result of the historical evolution of higher education. Higher education developed from religious institutions to philosophy until science emerged and broke the dominance of religion, philosophy, and the humanities.

This led to a clash between the humanities and sciences. The social sciences suffered from intellectual schizophrenia with members split between the two sides. By the end of the 19th century, the clash was resolved through an alliance between the humanities, the social sciences, and the natural sciences called liberal arts. While the three divisions continued to compete with each other, their leaders decided that aggregating across the three fields would get more students if each of the three required credit hours in their domain. Thus, the liberal arts core curriculum was born.

The history of higher education is like the history of Western religion where the development of various sects led to instability in the Catholic church and eventually a full-scale revolt and loss of members. It led to the Thirty Years Religious Wars which ended when the Catholics and Protestants decided to stop killing each other. Think of the Kingdom as the Catholic Church and the Protestants as the professional schools.

The Kingdom has survived but with fewer students and less authority in higher education. It is now in a crisis mode. Its supporters and faculty keep circling the wagons to protect market share and survival. Its core belief in scholarship continues to be the Kingdom's mantra. However, four major and non-reversible trends inside and outside the Kingdom are slowly changing the religion as much as the revolution started by Martin Luther.

The first trend started with the separation between liberal arts and the professional schools. This started in the late 18th century and has continued until the Kingdom only has about 30% of the undergraduates. It would have fewer students if there were more seats for students in professional programs. Some universities don't have more seats to meet demand because liberal arts faculty tend to have more friends in high places. As the process continues, they will be losing some of those friends if things continue as they are.

The professional undergraduate programs took off in the 20th century and became the archenemy of liberal arts education. It placed know-how above knowledge. The battle lines were formed between theory and application.

The second trend was the GI bills that have funded millions of veterans and their families since 1945 and continuing today. This resulted in the increase in the number of commoners in college who neither understood nor appreciated scholarship for its own sake.

The third trend was the explosion in the number of fields and undergraduate programs to recruit students and gain funding. The new degree and research programs were not originally accepted by the Kingdom, but pressure mounted thanks to the success of the Civil Rights movements. Women studies and African American studies programs kicked off the trend. New majors and minors along with certifications created many options that were relatively narrow in scope. They competed with each other, which has led to a more fragmented market for undergraduates. These programs multiplied, transforming the liberal arts core into a buffet of learning, as apologists for the Kingdom like to call it.

The Kingdom has suffered from tribalism from the beginning. The three major tribes are the sciences, social sciences, and the humanities. Within each of the three domains, the next largest set of tribes are the disciplines, and within each discipline there are sub-tribes as for example in Economics, macro and micro, which break into more sub-tribes. The Kingdom is no different from the religious institutions where religious sects emerge, grow, and disappear.

The tribalism within the Kingdom and religious institutions are similar to tribalism in all walks of life. In today's world, many tribes and sub-tribes within tribes and many sub-tribes within sub-tribes exist in all things human. The world has always been tribal. In the last two centuries, the total number of tribes and conflicts among them have increased because of the number of people and technology. Social media has played a major role in building the number of tribes and sub-tribes. The Kingdom is shattered into little pieces just like other institutions.

Fourth and most devastating for the sanctity of scholarship is the emergence of the Diversity, Inclusion and Equity (DEI later enlarged to DEIA by adding Accessibility) movement, and the attack on the traditional central theme of the Kingdom, the study of Western Civilization. The inclusion of non-Western culture as part of core requirements has reduced the emphasis on Western culture. History was rewritten to demonstrate that the Canon, which is a short-hand term for the focus on the West, was suspect. Driven by dissatisfaction by the societal conditions usually called "social justice," enough scholars have discredited the primary role of the Canon in undergraduate education.

This rejection of Canon was as devastating to the religion of the Kingdom as Martin Luther posting the 95 Theses was to the Catholic Church. There was no single leader, like Luther, but a series of scholars primarily from Philosophy and English and the new "disciplines" also joined the social sciences, taking down the focus on Western Civilization.

The book, *The Closing of the American Mind*, became a popular defense for restoring the Canon to its rightful place. The book, published in 1987, was a *New York Times* best seller for four months on the nonfiction list, and was written by a philosopher, Allan Bloom.[2] He was a dedicated scholar even as a teenager who believed that higher education should educate people to be like him.

His book complained about the failure of universities to educate its students, by which he met to treat them as scholars learning the Canon. The book suffered from getting off track with pro and con discussions over esoteric questions of philosophy. Going into the weeds is a cherished liberal arts practice. The book's point was about how the life of the mind should be the goal of university education.

The title advocates that scholarship should be the purpose of undergraduate education to counter the "Closing of the American Mind." The millions who read the book were elites from government, business, and the non-profits who thought scholarship was the path to leadership. Its popularity shows that many liberal arts true believers live outside the academy.

Those supporters who live outside of the Kingdom are alumni of the Kingdom's programs. They provide spiritual support for the Kingdom's administrators and faculty and contribute to the inflexibility of the Kingdom in promoting equity and inclusion. They reinforce the Kingdom's commitment to the sanctity of scholarship, especially when they make contributions to the Kingdom. Many liberal arts donors have made huge contributions in the form of getting their names on something or creating faculty chairs to study what they thought was worth studying. They donate because they want to be associated with the elite ideas of liberal arts.

Not all the intellectual elites were on Bloom's side. Many, especially in academia and the humanities and social sciences, liked the idea that there is a global society with many cultures, and none is inferior or superior to western cultures. They also thought there was too much mythology surrounding the Canon. They began to welcome DEI thinking and the battle lines were drawn.

When events in society like the several videos of police brutality against people of color went viral and dominated the media, many members of the Kingdom were emotionally motivated to not just present their views but to demand the liberal arts curriculum accommodate the reduction if not the elimination of the Canon. The stridency of these supporters of a broader approach to liberal arts began to challenge free speech norms, just like extreme and ardent supporters of the traditional canon did.

At risk was the sanctity of scholarship, the heart of the Kingdom's religion. The number of tribes and fields of study exploded with the intolerance of new tribes so that the concept of scholarship was under attack. The traditional view of John Stuart Mills and others that value free speech above all else was under attack, primarily in the form of not allowing conservative speakers on campus and focusing the content of courses against certain political groups.

These developments led to the basic challenge to the sanctity of scholarship by implying that the products of the scholarship of various tribes had a limited shelf-life rather than living forever. Did Plato, John Stuart Mills, or Isaac Newton really need to be studied if tribes at every level might like "newer" ideas? Consequently, the role of scholarship within the liberal arts curriculum is not about providing substantive knowledge that will stand up to the test of time but whatever the faculty decides is worth learning. The threat to the sanctity of scholarship is a crisis in the liberal arts religion because it is questioning the value of scholarship itself.

THE PATH TO EQUITY AND INCLUSION

The worship of scholarship cannot be the overriding and operational goal of undergraduate education. The goal should be, as already stated, the development of the student to be ready for life after college. That is what students, and their parents, are paying for. That is what a stable society and the reformed liberal arts needs for survival. Scholarship is valuable as a component of undergraduate education if it is a means to the end of a better life.

The belief that somehow exposure to the scholarship of the liberal arts core and mastering content at some level in a field or two in a liberal arts discipline will prepare students for life is a very hard sell to most undergraduates and the primary cause of distrust between faculty members and undergraduates.

Liberal Arts faculty need to adjust their commitment to making students scholars enough to help the students develop their own views in whatever area they want to, and to prepare for life after college. The question frequently posed to educators is, "Which do you care more about, your subject matter or your students?" That is a similar question Martin Luther asked of the leadership of the Catholic Church, "Which do you care more about, the church or your parishioners?"

The answer should be both. The Kingdom's commitment to the highest standards of scholarship needs to be maintained because they embody the idea of rationality. The life of the mind has an important role helping students to reject ideas with no empirical or logical base and to problem-solve through open discourse. But the Kingdom also needs to serve the needs of undergraduates in preparing for a world after graduation. The overemphasis on scholarship inherent in the bait and switch business model needs to be reduced. Scholarship and life goals of undergraduates need to be co-equal in importance. Without it, there will be no movement toward equitable and inclusive undergraduate education.

NOTES

1. "Homepage." *AAC&U*, https://www.aacu.org/. Accessed 28 Jan. 2023.
2. "Allan Bloom." *Wikipedia*, 4 Jan. 2023. *Wikipedia*, https://en.wikipedia.org/w/index.php?title=Allan_Bloom&oldid=1131424972.

Chapter 10

"Dumbing Down" Is Dumb

> The term dumbing down is subjective, because what a person considers as a dumbed-down cultural artefact usually depends upon the taste of the reader, the listener, and the viewer.
>
> —Pierre Bourdieu, *A Social Critique of the Judgement of Taste 1979*

Nothing reveals the Kingdom's elitism more than the constant vigilance against dumbing down and the ever-present fear of being accused of having made their course too easy. The accusation of dumbing down is so devastating that faculty members who might suspect a colleague is making their course too easy hesitate saying it to a faculty member. They may say it to other colleagues. The dumbing down bogeyman lurks everywhere.

The term itself implies that if someone makes a course easier to understand, either the students are too dumb to get the full shot, or the professors are not able to deliver higher level material. Readings might be reduced, or curves might be implemented to help what they see as the dumb students. When the faculty gets defensive about the dumbing down accusations, they see it as their standards being attacked.

In the meantime, even the most rigorous faculty members dumb down things in response to poor student performance, student survey results, guilt about equity, or the need to fill seats. Lindsey Rogers who was a visiting professor at John Hopkins from Harvard told his class that the Harvard graduate program would give Chinese students B's when they would have gotten a lower grade due to the language barrier. That was in 1959. Level of English skills continues to be a factor in the education of international students, but the accommodations are not called dumbing down. To do so in 2023 would be a massive micro-aggression.

When the questions of standards are brought up in the Kingdom, it is about the life of the mind and not life. It is about knowledge and not know-how. It's about figuring out what is on the professors' and other scholars' minds.

A major issue surrounding the concern about dumbing down is that the purpose of a liberal arts education is to create scholars, and if the arguments accepted throughout this book are taken seriously, it would require the Kingdom to have two purposes: scholarship and career preparation. The Kingdom's purists do not accept the second purpose on the grounds that "that is not what a liberal arts education is." If we accept the purists' position, the obvious conclusion is that the Kingdom should drop its bait and switch model and admit only those students that wanted to learn for the sake of learning and were capable of meeting the Kingdom's standards of scholarship.

One of the tools of dumbing down is the use of curves. Professors will give tests based on a hundred points, but the class average will be 52. They don't want to give half the class an F, so they curve where a 73 out of 100 is an A, for example. This reveals that those professors have no idea what their standards are and that they want to see who the best students in the class are. They want to throw as much scholarly mud against the wall and see what sticks. Students' performance determines the grade so dumbing down is presumed to be not the fault of the professor.

Some professors will tell the class, "I'm only giving one A" or will be happy to have a lower average grade because it "proves" that they are tough and have high standards. The students become the victims of the professor's ego. This behavior is far from inclusive or equitable.

No need to get into a debate over the pedagogical usefulness of curves even though there are scholarly publications on this question. Who would know anyway? The point is that the elitist approach to students learning leads to curves. It also raises the question whether or not the professors know what a good performance would be, so they leave it up to the grade distribution. How can they say they have standards?

Grade inflation is viewed as a form of dumbing down. High class or want-to-be high class colleges, not just in liberal arts, will have the faculty vote on the percentages of A's to be earned in a course. As the average GPA has gone up, the general conclusion is that all undergraduate education has been dumbed down. Requiring a bell-shaped curve for grades is a way to prove there is no dumbing down as measured by grades. This becomes a closed system where grades only measure grades and not what is learned.

For the Kingdom of liberal arts, grade inflation generates bad feelings between the natural sciences and mathematics on the one hand and the social sciences and humanities on the other. The natural sciences faculty feel that the other two divisions are getting better enrollment because they are easier. Of course, courses outside the physical sciences or math are easier to commoners who are allowed into the Kingdom but not interested in the life of the mind.

Another target of the dumbing down accusation is extra credit points where if students in history go to an outside lecture or a science course has extra credit research opportunities, they get points. The extra credit points are incentives just as curves are a form of incentive.

Implicit in the dumbing down attack on extra credit is that those students who are smart, which is assumed to be the opposite of dumb, will achieve the high standards without extra help. Extra credit is an incentive that requires more time on tasks for students, but time on tasks is not considered an acceptable measure of performance. The elitist view is that getting the right answer is more important than spending time on getting the right answer. When it comes to skills, practice is as important or more important than getting the right answer on tests.

We know that students who practice more and spend time on tasks perform better. This is particularly important in courses that have skills as a goal. Hard work is considered necessary by the Kingdom, but it is not enough. The Kingdom faculties refuse to accept time-on-task to be a major determinant, if not the sole determinant, of grades because only students like them deserve high grades.

The lack of appreciation for time-on-task can be found in the practice of many professors who refuse to take attendance or reduce student grades for missing classes. Unlike corporate and government training where attendance at training sessions is frequently the only standard, these professors consider performance on tests as the criteria of achievement. They know that students cram for exams and then probably forget what they theoretically learned but that apparently does not matter. From their elitist perspective, they would never see the failure to take attendance as dumbing down. From a time-on-task perspective, it obviously is.

A revealing glimpse of how dumbing down rankles the Kingdom is the work of Howard Gardner. He came up with the idea of multiple intelligences which was reacted to poorly by most members of the Kingdom because it was more than the life of the mind while using a cherished elitist word of the Kingdom, intelligence. He called for considering the following eight intelligences:

Spatial Intelligence
Kinesthetic Intelligence
Musical Intelligence
Verbal Intelligence
Intrapersonal Intelligence
Social Intelligence
Mathematical Intelligence
Naturalist Intelligence

What freaked the Kingdom out the most was the use of the word "intelligences" which was heretofore thought of as intellectual performance. How dare he use the "I word" when it is considered the criteria of what makes the elite. It sounded too much like know-how and not knowledge.

Gardner's Multiple Intelligences appealed to K–12 teachers and administrators because they know that the bulk of their students need to improve their skills in various areas. They know it because they worked closely with students and cared about their students' future. Members of the Kingdom with their arm's length relationship with students, the majority of which are commoners, just don't take responsibility for helping their students have success as the students define it.

Gardner's broadening of the term "intelligence" was a brilliant rhetorical tactic because it caught the members of the Kingdom by surprise in dumbing down what the word "intelligence" means. Some tried to rationalize it as part of liberal arts while others just dismissed it as fuzzy thinking.

THE PATH TO EQUITY AND INCLUSION

Pierre Bourdieu, a French Sociologist quoted at the beginning of this chapter, followed up his comment that "dumbing down" was subjective with a comment about its connection equity. "In a society in which the cultural practices of the ruling class are rendered and established as the legitimate culture of that society, that action then devalues the cultural capital of the subordinate social classes, and thus limits their social mobility within their own society." The Kingdom's emphasis on scholarship leaves many commoners at a disadvantage and unable to get many of its higher-level awards.

Faculty are on the lookout for faculty who are "too easy" and at the same time, they fear that they themselves will be labeled as such. "Dumbing Down" is a bogeyman that shuts down discussions of educational objectives and appropriate standards. It leads faculty to avoid the need to scaffold their courses and their curriculum which in turns disadvantages the commoners who are the majority of their students. It is an example of how the elitism of the Kingdom creates a barrier to equity.

Fortunately, Gardner's initial ideas are having an impact on K–12 education, especially in elementary schools using social emotional learning (SEL). SEL is defined as "the process through which children develop knowledge, attitudes, empathy, maintaining positive relationships, and making response decisions."[1] Although the practice makes most sense at the K–12 level, it needs to be taken seriously by college faculty at least in the first and second years. The Kingdom's faculty could not only provide the kind of support to build better attitudes among its students but could also help connect with its students. It could build trust between undergraduates and faculty members necessary for inclusion and equity.

NOTE

1. Amy L. Green et al. (Oct 2021). "Evaluation of the SPARK Child Mentoring Program: A Social and Emotional Learning Curriculum for Elementary School Students." *The Journal of Primary Prevention*, vol. 42, no. 5, pp. 531–47. *DOI.org (Crossref)*, https://doi.org/10.1007/s10935-021-00642-3.

PART III

Undergraduate Victims

How the costs to undergraduates imposed by the Kingdom outweigh the benefits they receive.

Chapter 11

Commoners Vote with Their Feet

They voted with their feet (regarding Russian soldiers deserting the army of the Tsar).

—Vladimir Lenin

The most convincing evidence of the harm done to commoners by the Kingdom is the decline in liberal arts enrollment, especially the humanities, compared to the increase in professional school enrollment, especially business. Unfortunately, finding data that compares liberal arts enrollment to non-liberal arts enrollment is difficult.

Anecdotal information about the closing of liberal arts colleges or their partnership with bigger universities exists. Many colleges have gotten rid of majors and even whole departments in the humanities because of the students' lack of interest.

While the humanities have clearly been declining for a while, there is less information about the other parts of liberal arts. However, the National Center for Education Statistics published a report which shows that the number of bachelor's degrees in social sciences and history have also declined 7% since 2009.[1]

Data from the National Center for Education Statistics shows that in 2019–2020, 20% of bachelor's degrees were in liberal arts, 53% were in non-liberal arts, and the remaining 27% were unknown and unlikely to be in liberal arts. In contrast to the decline in social sciences and history, between 2009–2010 and 2019–2020, business degrees increased by 8% and health related studies increased by 98%.[2]

This trend can be seen even more clearly in veteran students. Veteran students are more likely to be commoners than the rest of the student population. Their choices demonstrate the behavior of the larger population of commoners.

The Syracuse website on veteran enrollment for 2021–2022 shows that 27% of student veterans are pursuing business degrees, 14% are pursuing STEM degrees, and 10% are pursuing health degrees.[3] The business percentage especially is very telling. Veterans are more likely than the general population of students to have a commoner's point of view toward their education.

Why has there been this shift in trends? Many studies, including the National Center for Education Statistics, speculate that students are tired of college debt. They want a career that will get them a high starting salary so that they can start to pay off that debt right away. Professional schools seem less risky.

A significant trend in the loss of students in the Kingdom has been the reduction in males. This is part of a general societal trend where families want their daughters to go to college and much as their sons. However, the trend may be exacerbated by the heavy emphasis on the sanctity of scholarship in both college and high school. Female students tend to mature faster than male students. They also tend to do what they are told to do even though they may not buy learning for its own sake. Males tend to be bothered more than females by the lack of answers that make sense to the question "why do I have to learn this?" As of 2023, the trend is continuing and not likely to be reversed for liberal arts programs specifically.

Just as people move from high tax states to low tax states indicating they like to avoid taxes, the percentage of students who move from liberal arts to the professional schools reflects flight from poor opportunities to better opportunities. When businesses and nonprofits have a declining customer base, their first action is to increase marketing, and their second action is to rearrange deckchairs on the *Titanic*; they create new products out of their old products. Liberal arts programs do the same.

The leaders of the Kingdom would want to keep the emphasis on scholarship and theory above career preparation despite the loss of a customer base. This could only mean that they have been delusional about the decades long decline. They may look for joint programs with professional schools or to create new interdisciplinary majors by taking courses from existing majors and maybe adding an interdisciplinary course to provide cover. Despite these efforts, commoners continue to vote with their feet, taking their business away from liberal arts and towards the professional schools.

The Kingdom's decline, especially among males, is evidence of the gradual weakening of the Kingdom's bait and switch business model. The sanctity of scholarship with the related argument that the study of scholarship leads to leadership, creativity, and a good job is losing and will continue to lose market appeal. The availability at little cost of tools like the web and free online courses, the use of podcasts, and as the costs and requirements of liberal arts college grow, students increasingly satisfy their "love of learning" from non-academic sources.

The decline in the Kingdom's enrollment, which is higher for males and for veterans, demonstrates its lack of inclusion and contribution to equity. It demonstrates how the Kingdom has ignored the interests of large numbers of commoners.

THE PATH TO EQUITY AND INCLUSION

Commoners want the same thing that those in East Germany wanted before the walls came down, the desire for freedom. They want the freedom to have academic experiences that lead to a better life after graduation. More than 90% of the 120 credits needed for a college degree and a major are too constraining. Commoners see these requirements as hoops they must jump through to get the piece of paper to get a career.

The Kingdom needs to have a business model that helps students develop the skills they need for success through coursework while still providing experiences in working with what scholars do. The knowledge and wisdom of the academy must be combined with substantial development of the entire range of professional skills, such as experience with Microsoft Excel and people skills like teamwork. Only both avenues combined will lead to career success and a happy life. It is not enough to say that professional skills will be developed outside of academic credit as the Kingdom now says.

The Kingdom faces two challenges in this move to improve enrollment. First, it will have to embrace the professional development component with commitment and execution by the faculty. Second, it will take decades for future students and their parents to believe there is a new Kingdom. But the Kingdom has no other choice if it does not want to face lower enrollment.

NOTES

1. *COE—Undergraduate Degree Fields.* https://nces.ed.gov/programs/coe/indicator/cta/undergrad-degree-fields. Accessed 28 Jan. 2023.

2. *COE—Undergraduate Degree Fields.* https://nces.ed.gov/programs/coe/indicator/cta/undergrad-degree-fields. Accessed 28 Jan. 2023.

3. *Student Veterans: A Valuable Asset to Higher Education—D'Aniello Institute for Veterans and Military Families.* https://ivmf.syracuse.edu/student-veterans-a-valuable-asset-to-higher-education/. Accessed 28 Jan. 2023.

Chapter 12

The Anxiety Machine

Anxiety is the dizziness of freedom.

—Soren Kierkegaard

Students face all kinds of stressors as they progress through college. Stressors even start before college. As they move into the 9th grade, students are victims of multiple college-related stressors. They agonize over the big question of what they are going to do after high school and are they capable of getting into a "good" college. The stressors are overwhelming as parents, teachers, administrators, and guidance counselors contribute to the pressures to tie career success too closely to the "quality" of the college.

Considerable evidence exists that reports the high levels of anxiety among undergraduates. According to a study by the American College Health Association summarized by a Syracuse University official, 70% of college students say they have experienced overwhelming anxiety; 40% report experiencing moderate or severe psychological distress; and 25% have reported depression symptoms that affected their academic performance.

A top story for the year 2022, "A Stunning Level of Student Disconnection," published on 12/19/22 and identified by the Chronicle of Higher Education, talked about students' disconnection from the academics of higher education. This is one of many examples of discussions about how students have reduced their enthusiasm and time commitment to coursework. In the same issue, another top story was identified entitled "The Great Faculty Disengagement" which suggests unhappiness of the faculty.

Although anecdotal and referring to all of higher education, it is two pieces of evidence that the faculty and undergraduates in the Kingdom are not in a good relationship. Some blame it on COVID, but the relationship has been poor ever since the commoners became the majority of students. Living in a relationship where expectations are built on promises that are not delivered is a recipe for high levels of anxiety for both parties, especially students, and a major source of distrust.

Students who believe the advertising that college is necessary and have little idea of what is taught in college may have more anxiety than students from elite families. However, students from elites face their own set of stressors which might simply be defined as getting into a high enough ranked school to please themselves, their parents, their teachers, and their peers.

Once starting college, students fear they may not be good enough to graduate or to get a high GPA. Fear and risk are inherent in adult life, and students in their teens may not have good coping skills or adult advice to help limit the anxiety-producing effect.

Some, perhaps the majority of undergraduates in this country, see college as both a needed requirement for career success and a time for exploration or, to be perfectly honest, a time and place to have a good time. Many follow the path of Bart Simpson or Alfred E. Neuman from *Mad* magazine whose by-line was, "What, Me Worry?" They live in the present and give little thought to their future other than to fret about it. The fun-lovers may be the least prone to anxiety up to their senior year. They can ignore pressure from their family and other adults if they can change the subject when they are asked, "what are you going to do after college?"

While all teenagers are prone to anxiety over their educational futures, undergraduates in the Kingdom of liberal arts face more stressors. Some liberal arts students have their eye on graduate school. This goal creates the added pressure, as they did in high school, to perform well enough to get into a graduate program of their choice. For the liberal arts major, they can say "law school" when asked, "what are you doing after college?" They can also say medicine until they get a C- in organic chemistry.

Some may choose liberal arts as a default decision because they were not ready to decide on a professional school program or because they could not get into a professional school program. They see college as a step toward preparing for a happy life but are not sure how college will get them there.

Career confusion is rampant in the Kingdom because its educational mission is for students to gain scholarly skills and "knowledge" rather than professional skills. The typical statement made in the Kingdom's advising is, "it is not important which major you choose," quickly followed by, "so what's your major going to be?" Sophomores are encouraged, if not required, to identify a major by the end of their sophomore year.

If they ask about a major in a field, for example anthropology, they are told, "here's what kinds of jobs anthropologists get," even though the mantra of liberal arts is "you can do anything." The anxiety is caused by the confusion implicit in these statements. No wonder the majority of undergraduates say advising is not helpful. It is not the fault of the advisors but the fault of the bait and switch dynamic of liberal arts.

Commoners don't understand that their coursework is about learning what different scholarly tribes study. They may want to study politics, poetry, or chemical reactions, but they find themselves studying the disciplines of political science, literature, or chemistry. Any given course in this field has to do what scholars say. The best way to think about it is that they are studying the scholarship of the subject. They are "studying the study" of whatever field through the lenses of scholars rather than studying reality.

They are not studying, as discussed in Chapter 1, know-how. They are forced to study knowledge that is presented as theory rather than practice. In addition, if it is beyond the basic survey courses of the field, they will be studying the scholarship of a sub-tribe or sub-sub-tribe of that field. They are faced with lectures and readings that use the language of the scholars. If they can't understand that language, they are likely to think there is something wrong with them.

Commoners become frustrated with this treatment and usually change majors to find a field they can understand. They may reduce their interest in doing well in courses and lose themselves in other activities. Or they tune out. These behaviors are an indication of their desire to reduce their anxiety where they need to make decisions that shape their future but have no idea how.

In addition, the stress around the academic work itself prevents students from taking actions that will help them achieve their career goals. Many undergraduates who want to get a job or an internship will not have an up-to-date resume, maintain a LinkedIn, start looking for a summer internship in the fall, use career services, or explore job and internship search sites.

They are so overwhelmed with everything else, that even if they wanted to start looking for internships, they wouldn't know where to go. Their primary concerns are grades and degree completion, which frequently puts getting an internship or even thinking about their next step after graduation on the back burner. Having things on one's back burner may help in time management but does not reduce their overall anxiety of not knowing where they are going or how to get there.

The Kingdom's bait and switch model produces similar results as the approach/avoidance experiments psychologists like to do on rats. Rats learn to do something if rewarded with cheese and learn not to do something if punished with an electric shock. They become confused by alternating reward and punishment and don't know what to do, exhibiting anxious behavior.

Commoners in the Kingdom are put in the position of rats. The cheese is the promise of obtaining a viable career as a result of their college education, and the electric shock is academic work based on the sanctity of scholarship which they are not prepared for and didn't expect. If the undergraduates' primary goal is not the love of learning for its own sake, they are in a prison they don't want to be in, or they don't even realize they are in prison.

They learn that the best way to free themselves is partying, social life, drugs, alcohol, student activities, community service, going home to family every chance they get, and reducing the time they spend on academics. Surveys of students for decades show students increasingly spending less time on academics. These and many other activities relieve stress in the short run. The long run consequences may be even more stress.

An underlying factor contributing to undergraduate anxiety is what might be called "optionitis," the tendency to explore every option provided. They are like someone at the racetrack betting on all eight horses in the race. Optionitis is a universal disease thanks to advertising and living in a consumer society. The Kingdom brings academic optionitis to the undergraduates with changing courses, majors, minors, and ad hoc programming. Because each academic sub-tribe is fighting for more students, the incentive to slow down options doesn't exist, just like car manufacturers have no incentive to stop advertising new options.

Even what students see as the highly constraining liberal arts core provide what seems to be an infinite number of ways to complete it. It is not a core but an unlimited buffet of subjects. It's the Golden Corral on steroids. The defense of the unlimited buffet, especially for the liberal arts, is that it provides students the freedom to choose what they are interested in. However, the options are meaningless or irrelevant. They are theoretical and not know-how.

Most humanities and social sciences students see being forced to take X number of science courses as a loss of freedom, especially when courses that might interest them or seem to be less work and less difficult don't fill the science and mathematics requirement or are closed.

Freshmen particularly have a hard time with the core because they see it as high school all over again, and they don't see it as pursuing their interests or passion. The desire to pursue interests and passion is strong among first year students but usually ebbs as they realize they are not interested in becoming a scholar or going more in-depth beyond their current level of interest.

Better prepared students are able to do well because they are familiar with the liberal arts core requirements, or they don't even have to take them. Poorly prepared students are likely to come out of their first year with a GPA under 3.0. This tends to create a division among students into an upper class (3.5 and above) and lower class (below 3.0). The upper-class students brag about their GPAs to anyone who will listen, and the lower-class students try to hide it from everyone they know. As they talk to each other, the lower-class students wonder what's wrong with them, which helps to build a feeling of insecurity and therefore anxiety.

Academic optionitis is a source of anxiety for all students. The number of minors and majors has grown within liberal arts programs as the liberal arts departments chase enrollment. In addition to the creation of multidisciplinary majors, professional school programs are also chasing enrollment by offering minors or second majors. Students realizing that liberal arts doesn't help them career wise look to add professional school majors. This creates what seems to be an infinite number of programs and courses for students to consider.

Undergraduates rarely invest the time and effort to figure out what is going on and what options might be most useful. They need to get their 120 credits and fulfill liberal arts and major requirements. Added to that is that most of the faculty have limited knowledge of options. Professional advisors try the best they can to present options to students, but they have trouble keeping up with new courses and programs. Many of them in large institutions have caseloads bigger than high school guidance counselors.

The Kingdom is also big on options outside the set curriculum. It encourages opportunities to work with faculty on research projects, applications to prestigious scholarships like the Rhodes and Truman Scholarships, Study Abroad, and many other enrichment activities that may or may not generate academic credit and may or may not serve for career development. The Kingdom makes optionitis in extracurriculars which is where students go to escape the stress from their classes, so they are back to being stressed.

In pushing national scholarship awards, the Kingdom is creating even more options hurting both the elite students and the commoners. Elite students are encouraged to apply for the Rhodes and other scholarships which, if they do, will add a workload as much as a three-credit course while the odds of success are low. The pressure comes from the faculty of the Kingdom wanting to put notches in their belt and have reflected glory and from the elite students' need to win some evidence of self-worth. The Kingdom sees the awards as important for their branding to elite students who they chase with money and other amenities.

In the meantime, the commoners are wondering why they are not asked to pursue these scholarly awards even if they have relatively high grades. Intra-university scholarship awards based on outstanding scholarship do the same thing. Awards in public service or university service are always considered second class.

Beyond the academic alternatives offered by the Kingdom, undergraduates have many non-academic options like Greek life, student government, health clubs, and sometimes hundreds of student organizations. All of these opportunities can help them in the pursuit of a career path and may be more helpful than many of the Kingdom's academic courses. However, the Kingdom doesn't want to give academic credit because those opportunities are not in the life of the mind.

Most students, even commoners, know about the importance of networks for career and job searches so that gives them even more options to consider. They are looking for fulfillment and usefulness that they are not finding in their academic coursework, so they are more prone to pursue all of these activities.

Many of these opportunities build professional development skills, but they lead to burden and stress. Undergraduates have trouble organizing their priorities so that they can decide what to do and what not to do. Optionitis can lead students to missing deadlines, completing their tasks too quickly, or failing to deliver what they promise. Their grades may suffer, and they may wind up dropping courses, which may lead to taking courses outside the fall and spring semesters that create more costs.

The Kingdom contributes more to the anxiety of their students than just putting them in a perpetual approach/avoidance condition and providing unlimited academic and non-academic opportunities. The Kingdom places a set of expectations on undergraduates that are unrealistic. Undergraduates are told not only to live a life of accomplishment and be a leader but also to save the world. Recruiting sales pitches frequently promise the life of a leader. As discussed earlier, students and alums who had some achievements are used to promote a liberal arts education.

This marketing strategy plays on teenagers who suffer from the exuberance of youth. It is not uncommon for half of the political science majors to tell me they plan to be President of the United States. The sale of liberal arts as the path to becoming a great leader is both a cause and a symptom of stress. Students should view college as a rite of passage to engage in self-discovery and not as preparation to save the world.

High school and college graduation speeches place a burden on students to fix the world the current generations have screwed up. This sounds good at graduation events because it throws down a challenge. Since half the graduates are still suffering from partying the night before, they are fortunate that they are not listening. If they do listen, no wonder employers complain about the arrogance of the new college graduates.

The pressure for leading a life of accomplishment leads to another source of anxiety especially for liberal arts. In thinking about their passion and their careers they are confronted by the trade-off between doing good and doing well. Many of the students are preoccupied in high school by the ills of society, which the media does not let them forget. Much of the coursework in the social sciences and humanities reinforce this mind-set. Most liberal arts faculty members want their students to do good. They tend to be anti-business, which reinforces the anti-business attitudes of many liberal arts students. Faculty refer to students who leave English or Sociology to go to management school as going to the dark side.

As a result, liberal arts graduates frequently do not want to go into business, unless they are in liberal arts because the business school will not let them in. However, 85% of the job openings are in business rather than the nonprofit or government sectors.

Students who come to college with a passion to fix the world slowly come to realize that maybe they don't want the risk and lower pay associated with "do gooder" careers. They are in another avoidance-approach situation. The majority of students have figured out the trade-off and have taken a position by the time they are juniors that they have to do well enough to be able to do good. However, the path to that realization creates yet another stressor. Some students have not figured even by the time they graduate that, as the Zen cook says, you must feed yourself before you feed others.

Students who still want to do good are more likely than others to go to graduate school. Students who are not sure what they want to do might be helped by graduate schools even though the graduate programs claim they want students who have at least a general career focus. Graduate school for many students may be viewed as remedial because they haven't figured out their priorities yet thanks in part or in whole to career confusion generated by the Kingdom. This may help graduate school enrollments, but it may hurt the pocketbooks of undergraduates and their parents.

The Kingdom's anxiety-producing effects don't stop when the students graduate. The stigma attached to the lack of a college degree and specifically the lack of a liberal arts degree hurts undergraduates who did not complete their degrees or did not attend college. Dale Carnegie warned of this when he said, "I have talked to thousands of men who had inferiority complexes because they never went to college."[1] The stigma concerned Carnegie because he saw worry and stress as a growing problem in the modern world.

Many adults who have careers but who have not obtained a degree will have it on their bucket list. Some of these people are in viable careers but may perform less well in their jobs because they are spending their evenings or even time during their jobs doing online coursework. For those who succeed, their anxiety may be relieved. For the rest who have trouble moving on, they continue to be faced with pressure from themselves, their peers, or their family. Bucket lists are okay unless they get in the way of a happy life and good job performance.

THE PATH TO EQUITY AND INCLUSION

Administrators and faculty need to embrace the goal of reducing stress generated by the Kingdom. With all of the other pressures put on the faculty to change what they should do, this goal is rarely on the top of any administrator's list. Given that the faculty and the administrators themselves suffer from optionitis and the pressures from advocates of all kinds of things, there is little room for adding mental health as part of academic programming.

Although the entire college experience is an anxiety machine contributing to the many other stressors teenagers face in today's world, the Kingdom adds its own sources of anxiety. College administrators and faculty are aware of the growing mental health challenges undergraduates face. The actions they have taken so far are to increase mental health services on campus and create programs using undergraduates as peer advisors to help and offer advice through the media and meetings. They have also created "mental health" days which are in effect time-outs. These kinds of actions and programs may help, but more needs to be done.

They have not recognized the sources of stress they created through rules and regulations and the confusion created by the Kingdom's bait and switch business model. They have not asked faculty to design their courses with more clarity and more related to the students' experience. They may introduce faculty to the ideas behind Social Emotional Learning, as discussed in chapter 10, but they have not promoted those ideas like they have on DEI topics. An important first step would be to include ideas about how to promote mental health in their courses described by SEL.

Once that goal is accepted, the next step is to increase the one-on-one conversations between the undergraduates and faculty. The traditional approach is to have get-togethers with faculty members at dinner or for some occasion. This frequently results in few conversations with students and rarely works.

The old-fashioned view of a good relationship between a faculty member and a student was expressed in a quote attributed to the U.S. president James Garfield, who said that an ideal college was, "Mark Hopkins on one end of a log and a student on other end." Mark Hopkins was a theologian and president of Williams College in the 19th century.[2]

Some faculty, especially if they went to an undergraduate liberal arts program and sat on some log with a faculty member of their own, do not see that they were elite students whose love of learning gave them a connection to the faculty. They would never want to sit on a log with a commoner who went to college to get a career. The image or metaphor of professors and students sitting on a log is the opposite of inclusion.

While the most important thing that could be done to reduce the anxiety of undergraduates is for them to have a one-on-one relationship with a faculty member, a close second is to allow students to earn academic credit through professional development courses and opportunities. Most professional schools have an introductory course where skills and careers are discussed. The Kingdom has a broader challenge which is to offer academic credit for one or two of these general professional development courses.

NOTES

1. Steve Watts (2013), *Self-Help Messiah: Dale Carnegie and Success in Modern America.* Other Press.
2. Frederick Rudolph (1956), *Mark Hopkins and the Log: Williams College, 1836–1872.* New Haven: Yale University Press. *Internet Archive*, http://archive.org/details/markhopkinslogwi0000rudo.

Chapter 13

Career Services to the Rescue

> On rare occasions, as a career services director, I'd have a faculty member invite me into the class but always during the senior seminar class when—if they haven't done an internship or some real work by then—it's pretty much too late.
>
> —Heather Robertson, former director of
> career services at two universities

Career services staff members work to reduce the gap between the Kingdom's commitment to scholarship and the students' need to acquire the skills and explore careers during their college experience. The existence of career services and the considerable resources that support them show that the Kingdom does recognize the gap and responds to market forces. It's a baby step but not enough.

The Kingdom offers little academic credit to incentivize students to explore their careers and get the professional skills and experience they need. As a result, career services staff have to spend their time on outreach to students who are more focused on completing degree requirements than getting internships or taking job interest questionnaires. The majority of the Kingdom's faculty do not think a three-credit course on career exploration or internship and job searching strategies are worthy of liberal arts credit. As a result, the Kingdom prefers to call professional development and career exploration "co-curriculum" activities.

"Co-curriculum" is a revealing term. The Kingdom hopes that it will make it look like career support is part of the curriculum by giving it an official name. The idea has bounced around for decades about having some kind of document for co-curricular activities, something like an experiential transcript. The idea behind this thought is that employers would want to see a co-curricular transcript. Given the rigidities in the way employers make job decisions, that is wishful thinking. They tend not to look at transcripts anyway except to check the GPA and if the candidate actually graduated college. A second transcript with a name like "co-curricular" would even be less likely to be viewed.

Some progress in providing academic credit for career service coursework has been made. One-credit first year courses that teach students how to use career services are frequently offered, and the Kingdom is becoming more flexible on academic internship credit. These are important but small steps in the right direction. The Kingdom will herald these as big steps, but the students will not see it that way. So much material is thrown at them in such a short period of time during their chaotic first year that it is not enough to help them in their career exploration process.

The one-credit first semester courses, which are sometimes sold as helping in career preparation, are usually a hodgepodge, frequently diluted by other things like the marketing of programs abroad, mental health topics, and DEI content. Moreover, students don't usually do much work for a one-credit course because of its small impact on their GPA. If it were a three-credit course, students would work harder on a goal central to their interests.

The hesitation to commit academic credit for more systematic courses on professional development is the result of the commitment of the Kingdom to the life of the mind instead of to life. Willingness to view career preparation coursework as worthy of academic credit with one or two 3-credit courses would represent a sea-change in the thinking of the faculty.

The most substantial progress in providing academic credit has been the growth of internship opportunities. Students have increasingly been demanding academic credit for internships, and the Kingdom has responded to the pressure by making it easier for students to get credit. Chapter 14 describes the obstacles students face in getting experiential credit even though career services staff tries to help.

Career services staff, who have a heavy caseload of hundreds of students, are forced to combine advice on course selection for degree completion with career advice. These two tasks are difficult to accomplish in a 15 minute or even 30 minute conversation. Discussing the completion of degree requirements is concrete while career exploration is abstract. Moreover, much of the liberal arts degree requirements are based on the sanctity of scholarship which students have trouble connecting to professional development. Career service staff go out of their way to make the connection, but students are just confused further.

As a result, much of career advising takes the form of speaker series, alumni connection programs, advice, career interests surveys, and training on resume, interview, and job searching. Unlike the professional undergraduate programs where these sources are built into the curriculum, career service staff have to invest time and resources to convince students to take advantage of these programs during their free time. Time spent on marketing is less time spent giving students the tools they need to explore careers.

In addition, the administrators tend to nickel and dime the career services. They would much prefer to put dollars into adding more faculty and faculty research. Individual faculty may play a career advising role, but too often they are putting more of their effort into elite students who may make them proud someday. The faculty have trouble helping commoners pursue a career path who just want to have a nice life, a family, and be an asset to their community.

Lack of resources and uninterested students are compounded by the fact that the career advisors must advocate the ideology of liberal arts education in everything they say to make sure the Kingdom's brand is the centerpiece. The advisors repeat the liberal arts theme that students should be open to trying different things on the arts and science buffet to get all the skills they need to have a successful career. They say Liberal Arts will help them get internships, instead of just saying, "Career services will help you get your internships."

Career service leaders get pressure from various academic departments on needing more students. They face a conflict between populating all liberal arts courses and doing what is the best for the students. Courageous advisors will advise students to take courses in one or more of the professional schools, but they have to worry about a backlash if liberal arts enrollment goes down.

On top of recruiting and serving students, career services staff have market research tasks to add to their burden. They or others usually spend time and resources surveying students and alumni and gathering data on "employment rates" and "graduate school rates." These marketing activities are required to help reduce the negative effects of the Kingdom's bait and switch business model.

THE PATH TO EQUITY AND INCLUSION

The Kingdom has been slowly allowing career services and professional development to play a bigger role in the education of its undergraduates. It is almost as if the members of the Kingdom are holding their nose as they add resources and programs to career services. The Kingdom needs to accept the mission that career development is an essential part of its formal academic program. It needs to provide more resources and to create at least two 3-credit courses required of all students to prepare them for the skills they will need to pursue a career path other than academics once they graduate college. One of the courses should be a basic course early in the student's career and the other should be an internship course. Not only will these reduce the gap between the bait and the switch of the Kingdom, but it will also help promote citizenship skills, a goal claimed by the Kingdom to be paramount.

The role of the faculty in the development and delivery of these courses is complicated by the fact that the commitment to scholarship reduces their desire to offer such courses and to provide career advising. Some progress is being made, but the worship of scholarship stands in the way of a deeper commitment to professional skills in the Kingdom's curriculum.

Chapter 14

Experience Credit Ambivalence

For the things we have to learn before we can do them, we learn by doing them!

—Aristotle

Most undergraduates know that internships lead to work experience, an improved resume, skill development, and career exploration. For commoners, that is why they came to college in the first place. The demand for such experience in the Kingdom is high. The Kingdom's faculty members, and to a lesser extent administrators, are ambivalent. They prefer not to give academic credit for experience unless it complies in some way with their belief in the sanctity of scholarship.

Nothing illustrates the Kingdom faculty's belief in the life of the mind more than its lukewarm, if not hostile, attitude toward experiential credit. The sanctity of scholarship that drives liberal arts faculty fuels a reluctance to give academic credit for experience outside the classroom. Many faculty members believe experience credit is a form of dumbing down since it is about life and not the life of the mind.

The Kingdom most readily accepts academic credit for students working with faculty on research projects. Working with select students on a faculty member's research project guarantees that students will be on the proper road to be a scholar. It also gives the impression of maintaining academic rigor.

The problem with this preference is that it will usually appeal to the strongest students who may want to become scholars. It has value by having students do something for a boss rather than assignments for a professor. Other than that, any tools that might be picked up won't help students who want to do something other than research or academics. Experience credit based on working with faculty-based research projects is far from inclusive. In fact, because it is one more thing subsidizing the well prepared and academically oriented students over the commoner, it might be called exclusive.

Commoners are not likely to find this option for experience credit useful or appealing unless the research requires mastering tools that are used in 99% of the jobs outside of academics. Microsoft Excel or using commercial databases, for example, would be a good thing. Even entering data could help inexperienced students get their first internship. However, most research internships with faculty don't provide general skill development other than dealing with a boss.

As a result, commoners usually have a tough time getting experience credit that would help them explore career options or develop skills. Undergraduates who are commoners and not the apple of the faculty's eye, have problems finding a faculty member to authorize an experiential credit course.

Faculty members view offering an internship as a good use of their time if the experience is related to their field of study. A faculty member in a field such as chemistry would not want to supervise a chemistry student working at a community center because it has nothing to do with chemistry. The chemistry major wouldn't know other professors in more relevant fields, and even if they did, the professor would still probably say no. Professors say no in general because it is extra work, and also because they are members of the Kingdom, so they think they only have competence to give credit to students who are in their field of expertise.

Faculty giving research experience credit themselves are ambivalent. On the one hand, they would want the student to understand the theoretical concepts to justify academic credit. On the other hand, that would require the faculty to spend a lot of time for one student in designing and evaluating activities as well as coaching the student on the theory. This leads to the well-known and consistent faculty practice that might be called the academic two-step. It can be summarized by the statement: "I want students to do it right, but I don't have the time to spend on making sure they do it right, so I decline."

The academic two-step is practiced by faculty in other areas like how they avoid spending more time with students and creating new courses that students want. The two-step is caused by the faculty member's desire to appear to give higher priority to things like curriculum and spending time with students, but they don't have the bandwidth to do it "right."

About 15 years ago, the liberal arts dean at Syracuse University wanted me to talk to the natural science faculty about how to incorporate community service into their courses. I suggested that natural science courses for non-science majors provide credit for students to tutor chemistry or biology in high school. The response from the department chairs was "no" because high schools do not teach the correct science. In other words, the scholarship of high school science teachers was not good enough.

I countered, to no avail, that professors could use class discussion to explore the differences between their courses and what is taught in high school. It might provide a more interesting way to help commoners who were taking the science course as a lower division requirement to practice scientific reasoning. The counter appears to have been too much out of the framework of what the science chairs view as science education. The sanctity of scholarship is always a primary source of tension when it comes to experiential education.

In addition to the faculty's lack of interest in promoting internships, the Kingdom's faculty resist giving academic credit for experience credit hours where the student gets paid. Apparently, getting paid is enough of a reward and getting credit should not be a bonus. The aristocrats of liberal arts consider their academic credit so valuable that it is enough reward for commoners, no matter the undergraduate's economic status.

Professional skills like time management, people skills, and problem-solving might be okay for professional programs but not for the faculty in the Kingdom. They would prefer that experience credit lead to creative thinking rather than to the improvement of skills necessary for the workforce. Therefore, the few times faculty give credit, the assignments that are not directly related to scholarship are related to self reflection and thinking about things like citizenship and employers' ethics. It rarely rewards the students showing up on time or a supervisor's evaluation that students did a great job entering data. Such a standard would be trivial for the Kingdom's faculty even though it is key to getting and succeeding in a job.

Being responsible appears to be not worthy of academic credit but thinking about responsibilities would be. Even though the Kingdom's faculty would embrace responsible behavior, especially of citizens, the actual measure of showing up would not be considered a measure of responsibility. This viewpoint by the Kingdom's faculty members demonstrates the bias toward the life of the mind rather than life that is at the heart of the ambivalence toward experience credit.

Community service could lead to more academic credit than it does now. It is typically not given academic credit because it is an act coming from the heart and not the mind. Unless it can be incorporated in a course that has academic goals, which increasingly happens, community service is not worthy of academic credit.

There is an added complicating barrier for community service. Most of the Kingdom's faculty consider community service a practice in citizenship instead of it being useful to career and skill development. They rarely recruit students on the grounds that it will provide work experience or career and skill development. Besides not wanting to give out their precious academic credit, the Kingdom views community service as an act of altruism. The value in altruism is wanting to help others, so they don't feel like they should give other incentives for it. Commoners know that the act of altruism helps people feel good, so it is in itself in the altruist's self-interest.

A sociologist once said to me that he was against community service to nonprofits serving the poor but not on grounds that it wasn't academic. He surprised me by making a Marxist argument that helping the poor will slow down the destruction of capitalism even though it was helping the poor in the short run. This is a good example of theory and abstraction taking over educational treatments.

In addition to community service, student activities are a powerful form of experiential education that could be much improved by providing academic credit and focusing on professional development. For example, resident advisors (RA) who received extensive training for a very difficult job that is beyond a first job in many corporations may receive one credit. If the Kingdom embraced the need for undergraduates to have career development experiences, the number of hours spent in training and in practicing a whole range of professional skills would deserve three or six academic credits. It would also reduce the RA's course load, providing them time to do better in their other courses and reducing stress. This would be especially useful for students' pocketbooks and therefore a step towards equity and inclusion.

University employment, whether working in food services or as a tour guide, in addition to resident advisors, also involves training and practice that might be deserving credit. However, because it's a job, it's not usually accepted. Administrators and faculty in universities still have the attitudes of the Kingdom no matter where they are.

Another source of experience credit that could help students develop their professional skills is provided by student activities and jobs. Credit is rarely given to students who spend ten or more hours a week for a student organization. For example, the president of a student government is meeting with high level university officials while trying to maintain order among the rest of the members. Students working in food services that do such a superior job are promoted to supervisor which involves financial and people management, similar to what they would do in their post-college job, and they should receive credit. However, the Kingdom's faculty would not consider this to be developing the life of the students' minds.

Despite the powerful impact student activities could have on helping students prepare for life, there are many obstacles. The student activities advisors face many barriers. The first barrier is there is not enough staff to really give the attention that is needed to the hundreds of student organization leaders on many campuses. The second barrier is that they either don't have or won't use leverage to incentivize good behavior. For example, student organizations that missed deadlines are frequently allowed to submit things late. The third barrier is that the student activities staff frequently come out of the Kingdom, and they talk about leadership and other highly abstract terms instead of providing very specific guidelines. Training on how to run meetings, for example, "end meetings on time," "have a clear agenda for a meeting," and "send in financial information at the deadline," could help develop the skills of students.

The energy, interest, and attention span of most students, especially commoners, are greater for student activities than for academic activities. This means they are more open to learning information and practicing the skills they need for career success. If the barriers outlined above were to be reduced and these experiences were given academic credit, student activities could be an even more important venue for learning both content and career skills vital to their futures. Students would be more motivated to engage with them.

THE PATH TO EQUITY AND INCLUSION

The ambivalence toward giving credit for experiential education continues to limit opportunities for career development in most liberal arts programs, but the barriers are starting to dissipate as a result of the increasing demand of students. One strategy is to provide credit through writing programs where students can do whatever they want and write some reflection papers to satisfy the provision of credit. Other programs have practicum courses where students individually or in groups provide research and other services to clients in the community.

Co-op programs where students do a semester or two semester-long full-time internship experience exist in some, not many, institutions of higher learning. These types of formal programs are usually not in the Kingdom's programs. Even universities with co-op programs have trouble getting buy-in from the Kingdom. A source who works in the Kingdom and does not want to be identified told me that the liberal arts faculty at a co-op institution he worked for would not provide academic credit for a course or two to prepare students for their full semester-long co-op placement. This incident demonstrates the deep-seated antipathy to using credit for professional development even in programs designed to generate professional development.

Internships, community service, and student activities need to have more staff resources and to be more structured. Academic credit as well as additional staff would make this possible and enhance the skill development and career exploration of these activities. The staff that run student employment and student activities try to promote professional development but don't have the bandwidth to do it.

But "times are a changin." Both equity and inclusion would be well served if more ways are found to offer academic credit and more resources are devoted to making these experiences rigorous without going off the academic deep end. The rigor would come from careful monitoring of the student's internships or activities and the supervisor's evaluation. This does not only require innovative curriculum design, but it does require faculty spending time coaching students. It would also lead to building a more trusting relationship between undergraduates and faculty.

Most of all, the Kingdom must provide more internship opportunities and require it for degree completion either across the liberal arts curriculum or within each major. Students need to be coerced to develop skills and take internships even as they claim there are not enough opportunities. The only way to do it is to provide some room in course requirements where grades will motivate practice and performance.

PART IV

Societal Damage

How the Kingdom has damaged American Society.

Chapter 15

K–12 Toxicity

> When I think back on all the crap I've learned in high school. It's a wonder I can think at all.
>
> —Paul Simon, *Kodachrome*

The Kingdom's bait and switch business model has done more damage to the K–12 education system than it has done to undergraduate education. About five times as many students are in the K–12 system compared to higher education, so the scope of the damage is much greater. The K–12 curriculum has been dominated by the Kingdom's liberal arts coursework creating an education that is less useful to the vast majority of students. Public Education is supposed to be for the commoner, but its curriculum is for the elite.

Beyond discussing the Kingdom's direct curriculum damage to K–12 education, the greatest overall damage to American society is its relentless opposition directly and indirectly to vocational education in America. The damage to society is a result of the overselling of the liberal arts and by implication, the underselling of career preparation, from Kindergarten to High School, by the elites who decide on curriculum. The lack of vocational and career education has resulted in shortages in many fields including medical and many trade jobs.

The Kingdom's leaders don't see education as workforce policies but as policies to unleash the human spirit and create responsible citizens. This elitist viewpoint permeates debates among those in the education business as if the Kingdom had no customers and no political responsibilities. K–16 schools ask for help from businesses to either give them money or internships, but they don't want to make accommodations that the businesses would prefer in the curriculum. Like "war is too important to be left to the military," as the World War I French prime minister Georges Clemenceau said, the educational curriculum is too important to be left to an educational establishment dominated by the Kingdom. Unfortunately for American society, the Kingdom has had a stranglehold on most of K–12 education. The hold is weakening as the consequences become clearer, but change will be slow.

High school counselors encourage students to take high school courses shaped by liberal arts because they think, rightly or wrongly, that traditional liberal arts coursework is what college admissions officers want to see. Many counselors, school administrators, high school teachers, and parents view business courses as Plan B and vocational courses as Plan C only to be used by their students who can't do the liberal arts courses, especially math and science. That more high school graduates go to professional programs than liberal arts programs doesn't seem to matter to guidance counselors.

Looking at state high school degree requirements like the MCAS in Massachusetts and the Regents in New York State as well as the course requirements will demonstrate the dominance of the Kingdom's devotion to scholarship. Math courses up through Algebra 2 are required, and the "good" students are encouraged to take calculus. Statistics may or may not be required, and if taught, it is usually about formulas and theory. Math is taught as an art form instead of as a tool. Language is taught as learning about the culture and literature of a country instead of a tool to communicate. The high school curriculum mimics the Kingdom's college curriculum where knowledge is more important than know-how.

The dominance of the Kingdom in high school education results from the fact that most teachers come from liberal arts as do members of the school board and administrators. Most of these people think education is liberal arts and vocational programs are essential to public education. Efforts to make the curriculum more relevant and to include workforce preparation have had some influence but not enough to get proper funding and support from those in charge. The focus on career readiness has increased slowly and fitfully over the past four decades. The need for the change should not have been required in the first place, but the Kingdom ruled.

The Common Core, which was created to make K–12 education even more liberal arts, could have increased the toxic role the Kingdom plays in high school education if it had succeeded. Politicians and nonprofits supported the Common Core, like the "Council of Chief State School Officers which represents the top K–12 education officials from all US states and territories" and the National Governors Association. Several associations like Achieve, a nonprofit education reform group, the two major teachers' unions, the National Education Association and the American Federation of Teachers also supported it. National organizations based on disciplines like Math and English jumped on board.[1]

Around 2010, 43 state legislatures in different ways "adopted" the common core. The initial support demonstrates the stronghold that the Kingdom has among academic and political elites.

The Common Core supporters claimed that it would better prepare students for college and careers. The use of college and careers together is the same bait and switch practice of the Kingdom. Since less than 35% of people over 25 have a college degree, why are "college" and "careers" given equal weight? This coupling of the two terms leads readers to think that all careers require what colleges demand when in fact the majority of high school graduates don't go to or complete college. The Common Core is only about liberal arts college preparation.

Supporters of the Common Core movement felt that the standards and performance of students in many states were below those in other states. New York educators for example would identify the state of Mississippi as having standards below par. They blame this on the backwardness of members of school boards in that state. The Common Core movement was the opposite of regional inclusion unless the term "inclusion" meant all states must follow what the elite wants.

In addition, Common Core supporters would cite comparisons on international tests where United States students were far from the top list of countries. The generalizations that education should be uniform throughout the United States and that the United States should be at the top of the international academic achievement competition make perfect sense to the Kingdom. To anyone who looks at the massive socio-economic differences within the U.S. population and the homogeneity of the countries that beat the United States in the international academic testing wars, it makes no sense. The supporters played the public and the politicians knowing that international competition would drive support.

The same hubris and elitism that dominates the Kingdom played itself out in the creation and initial support of the Common Core movement. The movement was almost dead by 2020, because of a widespread grassroots rebellion. Politicians who needed the votes of commoners to win elections objected. Public hearings were packed, and parents objected to the tone-deaf position of the Common Core proposals that ignored the needs of their students. Local and state governments resented what they saw as top down demands from the federal government. They objected to new standards and new curriculum and more testing. The parents who supported the Common Core were outnumbered by the commoners who opposed it. Even if there had been no opposition, the cost and complexity of implementing the plan would have caused it to eventually collapse under its own weight.

The thinking behind the movement was typical of the Kingdom's worship of scholarship and abstraction. It was based on the nostalgia of those who want to return to the good old days of education which was designed for the elites of America who wanted the rest of America to be like them. The increased use of standardized testing, which the implementation of the

Common Core would require, would test whether or not students had gained the knowledge considered necessary.

If the Common Core movement had succeeded, it would have further increased the elitist and toxic nature of K–12 education. The Kingdom's dominance has already done enough to deprive commoners of an education to prepare them for life.

To illustrate how pernicious the effects of the liberal arts dominance of K–12 education are, one only needs to read the standards on Mathematics in the Common Core curriculum.[2] The topics identified and terms used are those that only mathematicians use to talk to each other. Instead of providing practice in high school for the most commonly used concepts like percentages, ratios, and statistical terms, the standards introduce more abstract topics like trigonometry, quadratic equations, and calculus. The Kingdom's focus on covering more and higher-level materials is not skills-friendly and therefore not helpful to the bulk of students who seek know-how rather than scholarship of mathematics.

The consequence of this is that the curriculum produces a majority of high school students who are math phobic with little experience in the majority of mathematical functions used in business, government, and the nonprofit world. In addition, those that can handle the scholarship of mathematics are rewarded regardless of their ability to problem-solve in concrete terms for the real world. And while the scholars are getting rewarded, those who can't participate in this scholarly game have more limited chances for merit aid than the many other opportunities given to the high math performers.

The degree to which liberal arts has dominated K–12 education has led to some people saying that they prefer to talk about K–16 education. It is as if college is the needed extension to high school. K–16 assumes that everyone has to go to college because a high school education is not enough for every American.

The Department of Education which is more open-minded about other courses than liberal arts courses and also more open about creating an education system where students do not have to go to college has used the term "postsecondary education." However, this term has not caught on because this sounds too much like vocational education which supporters of the Kingdom would find distasteful.

Competition for highly ranked colleges and universities is a powerful force in shaping students and parents' choice of coursework in high school. The colleges and universities that have a liberal arts reputation are the most highly ranked in *U.S. News and World Report*. Eighteen of the top twenty are known for their liberal arts programs. The criteria are set up to favor liberal arts institutions. Because students want to get into these highly ranked institutions, they are more likely to feel pressured to take liberal arts courses.

The Kingdom's pundits who insert themselves into K–12 education do so to push their own elitism. Jonathan Kozol wrote a book, *Savage Inequality*, which correctly pointed out the lack of funding for schools in poor areas in the 1980s. His writing and other people's led to court cases in which states were to equalize funding to counteract the effects of property taxes in paying for education. Yet when Kozol spoke in public, he frequently mentioned that we need an educational system where no matter what the economic status of the individual, all students should reach their potential to be great poets.

Would commoners see becoming a great poet as part of the American Dream? He and others would say, "yes." An education system with the goal of making students into poets is elitist and far from inclusive. All students who graduate high school need to know how to use percentages, but they do need to be great poets or even poets.

The Advanced Placement courses available through the College Board have reinforced the influence played by the Kingdom in K–12 education. Thirty-one out of thirty-four courses listed on the 2022 College Board website are traditional liberal arts courses. Added to the Advanced Placement program are courses offered by colleges, including community colleges, for college credit. These courses also tend to be primarily traditional liberal arts courses. The liberal arts dominance of these college credit courses speaks loud and clear that education is about the life of the mind even as many students are turned off by high school education because they don't see its usefulness.

In the name of equity, many high schools and some funders have waived the AP fees for students in poor areas. Commoners are allowed to think that taking AP courses would generate college credit when in fact less than 50% get a 4 or 5 on the test.[3] Taking AP courses is a distraction that could lead to lower performance in other classes while convincing poor performing students that they should go to college. While equity may be the rationale, the consequence is to hurt rather than help students who come from families in poverty.

The International Baccalaureate (IB) movement in the United States is also heavily dominated by liberal arts. Many schools adopted the IB program in whole or in parts which further created a market for liberal arts coursework in high school. The IB model came out of Europe with its focus on traditional liberal arts. It was touted as a way to raise standards, and it took resources away from traditional programs, both of which did not benefit the vast majority of students.

An important way that the Kingdom has influenced the curriculum of K–12 education is through disciplinary associations that influence the content of the curriculum. The mathematics lobbies have done enough damage to the teaching of new mathematics that parents can't help their children with their math homework, even if they have a college degree or higher. The mathematics curricula do not focus enough on the use of statistics as a tool because statistics itself is viewed by many mathematicians as not "real math." When they do teach statistics, they don't have students work with real data on real topics but on formulas behind the statistics.

If mathematicians could define their role as teaching quantitative analysis, high school students would be much better off. Microsoft Excel would be introduced in middle school or before. Students who graduate high school would be much better prepared for the workforce whether or not they go to college. As it stands now, many college graduates are not introduced to Excel in academic coursework. The impact of the Kingdom on high school has not led to equity and inclusion.

First, the college credit courses require resources that might be better spent on helping all the students pursue a path that suits their interests and their capabilities. Vocational and career and technical education programs could use more funds and more leadership support.

Second, the liberal arts dominance drives students' competition to get into ranked colleges. This competition further reinforces the liberal arts even though the bulk of the students taking AP courses are motivated by the goal of getting a good job.

Third, the academic focus on liberal arts rewards students who live and excel in the life of the mind. This focus punishes students who have many other qualities that are just as, or more important, for their entire future. This reward starts in elementary school as schools practice *de facto* tracking.

Fourth, this focus on scholarship creates a divide that generates hostility between scholarly and the non-scholarly students. The scholars tend to think they are going to be winners, and the non-scholars may or may not buy that, but they are resentful at the scholars' arrogance. The result of this is a *de facto* segregation in coursework as well as social activities between scholars and the non-scholars. Teenagers are vulnerable and easily buy the message that they are somehow not good enough. The development of gifted courses and the backlash against them illustrates the disruptive impact of liberal arts.

This is not necessarily an argument against honors or gifted programs. These programs make sense to serve students who are good at academics. What doesn't make sense is the heavy investment in these programs at the expense of more programs that serve all students. The Kingdom acts as a pressure group on K–12 education that determines the allocation of resources to programs serving the elite students.

Fifth, when students ask the question, "why do I have to learn this," no reason makes sense to them other than, "you have to get a good grade," which implies, "to get into college." This question and answer are at the heart of the reason why many students can't bring themselves to do the scholarship that is demanded of them in school. The Kingdom can't give a rational reason to its students, and neither can those running the K–12 systems. Parents and students will accept the answer to why students have to learn scholarly stuff "to get into college," because they would never ask "why do I have to get into college."

Sixth, students who have a passion for things like theater, music, and art, whether taught in classes or as student activities, are frustrated by the need to spend more time on liberal arts academics. This frustration over the trade-off of student activities and academic work, as already mentioned, explains why college students tend to prefer these activities over academic activities. The same dynamic exists at the high school level.

Poor graduation rates in high schools are caused by many factors that have nothing to do with the liberal arts bias of the curriculum. However, the liberal arts bias of the curriculum enhances these other factors. Given the distaste for these academic activities, especially in middle school and then high school, many students may decide to drop out of the school system because of the curriculum. If the curriculum had more hands-on teaching of tools, perhaps these potential dropouts would remain in school. This forecast is not and cannot be tested. It is based on what high school students say.

Teachers may also be harmed by the liberal arts bias. They love the liberal arts and want to help students enjoy it, but they're working with many students, if not the majority of students, who don't enjoy it. The same tension in college where the faculty and students don't trust each other exists in high school. This tension could lead to them leaving the teaching position or seeking to get an administrative position. Their liberal arts bias also leads them to leave schools in disadvantaged areas and go to the schools that they think have scholarly students.

Schools of Education usually require many liberal arts credits which bias potential teachers in thinking they will be able to teach liberal arts courses in high school. The liberal arts requirements predispose teachers to see that education is the love of learning and guarantees generations of teachers with that bias.

In contrast, those teachers who want to join the profession to help students who may not excel at traditional academic coursework are required to take that coursework and are frequently required to go to graduate school on the subjects as well as take tests for credentials that focus on the scholarly enterprise. One of my students who taught math to ninth graders finally quit because when students asked her why they had to learn the quadratic equations, she had no answer. She would have much preferred to teach them about credit card interest rates.

This discussion is not new. The struggle over the purpose of education and what to teach is centuries old. Curriculum decisions are political decisions that cannot be resolved through intellectual discourse. The proponents of the Kingdom need to become more inclusive in their viewpoint or weaker in the power they have over the curriculum.

THE PATH TO EQUITY AND INCLUSION

If the Kingdom's faculty members want to claim that it is committed to equity and inclusion, it needs to help K–12 educators serve the needs of all of its students, not just those who may go to college. The disciplinary associations that lobby for curriculum change under the "goal" of bringing what is taught into high school "up to date" need to have a view that is not bound by their narrow definitions of scholarship or their professional self-interest.

Inherent in the Kingdom's approach to education is to try to find new content to teach and new perspectives. This approach may be okay for college education, but K–12 education needs more stability. The Kingdom's faculty is so distant from K–12 education that it should stay out of content curriculum development. Curriculum change driven by the research of the Kingdom creates enough chaos for college students. At the K–12 level where students are less able to deal with changes in the curriculum, the impact is more serious.

The Kingdom as well as the Schools of Education have glorified the idea of research-based educational strategy. The brand "research-based" assumes there is a solid knowledge base for advocating a particular educational method. Evaluation research may be useful, but it should not be oversold as it is by the term "best practices." There can never be a legitimate claim that a teaching method is a "best practice." It would imply for a given practice that all strategies were studied, and performance measures yielded conclusive evidence. With no clear evidence of a best practice, the Kingdom should discourage its faculty members to tell the high school teachers what to do based on the tentative research it generates. Teachers need to adapt and understand their students, which is the first and most important step to inclusion. They don't need the Kingdom's faculty members telling them what to do no matter what they think their research shows.

If the Kingdom's faculty members want to play a more positive role in K–12 education, the basic concepts from the Social Emotional Learning (SEL) movement discussed earlier in Chapters 10 and 12 should be studied and practiced by the Kingdom's faculty. Some K–12 schools are using some of the strategies while almost no courses in the Kingdom do. If the Kingdom was able to convince its faculty members to approach their course design and students from the SEL perspective, it could help the high school. As long as the Kingdom's faculty members encourage high schools to put more of the latest scholarship in the curriculum, more of the students' time will be spent on the life of the mind and less on life.

NOTES

1. *AP Score Distributions—AP Students | College Board.* https://apstudents.collegeboard.org/about-ap-scores/score-distributions. Accessed 28 Jan. 2023.

2. *Everything You Need to Know about the Common Core—Vox.* https://www.vox.com/2014/10/7/18088680/common-core. Accessed 28 Jan. 2023.

3. *Common Core State Standards—National Council of Teachers of Mathematics.* https://www.nctm.org/ccssm/. Accessed 28 Jan. 2023.

Chapter 16

Unskilled Citizens

> Self-government is not possible unless the citizens are educated sufficiently to enable them to exercise oversight. It is therefore imperative that the nation see to it that a suitable education be provided for all its citizens.
>
> —Thomas Jefferson

In 2000, I found myself on *Larry King Live* discussing my book, *How You Can Help: An Easy Guide to Doing Good Deeds in Your Everyday Life*. I answered King's question, "Why did you write this book," by saying "to provide people with citizenship skills." He said incredulously, "citizenship skills?" No wonder Mr. King was incredulous. Most discussions of citizenship are highly abstract discussions about freedom, order, and equality—those are abstract feelings. In this day and age, citizens need more than abstract concepts and emotion. They need skills.

Twenty-two years later, the incredulity continues. Among conservatives, citizenship education is mostly about institutions and the constitution. Among liberals, citizenship education is mostly about social justice. Skills continue to be ignored.

The content is shaped by the never ending struggle between realists and idealists. The idealists are winning with our teenagers as one would expect of the young and naïve. As long as the goals of citizenship education are about content, they tell our students what to think and act; not how to think and act.

The "office of citizenship," as some scholars have called it, requires the same skills needed for success in any career field and given the nature of contemporary life in America, for all of life's challenges. The skills used by physicians, teachers, business executives, government workers, and all fields include people skills, information gathering skills, and an open mind that was at one time associated with the methods of science.

The skills of citizenship include teamwork and good written and oral communication skills that are essential for all successful professional careers.

These skills are necessary so that citizens build solid relationships with each other that will lead to the compromise required for good decisions in a democratic society.

Anyone who has ever attended a City Council, School Board, or Town Hall meeting knows how such skills are in very short supply and how politicians can use the absence of these skills to their advantage even as we sometimes wonder if the politicians themselves have such skills. Practicing Dale Carnegie principles may be more important for a functioning democracy than understanding the constitution.

Citizens also need to have the ability to gather information, use simple quantitative skills like percentages, ask and seek answers to the right questions, and problem solve. These skills should be at the heart of the mission of education in any democratic society. Citizens need them when they vote or try to influence politicians.

Citizens have to seek up-to-date and vetted information to check the facts provided by politicians, governmental officials, other citizens, and lobby groups. They have to make sense out of numbers and simple statistics. When a politician says the tax rate has gone down, the citizen needs to understand that taxes may not have gone down.

Asking and answering the right questions is even more critical. To do so requires detecting nonsense, paying attention to detail, applying knowledge to specific questions, and evaluating actions and policies. Problem-solving skills enable citizens to ask supporters of a new policy, "what's the problem and how do you know it exists," a useful exercise for all when a policy is under consideration. Without these skills, citizens are at the mercy of those who use rhetoric in the place of reason.

These skills are also critical for more than the citizen's role in shaping public policy or voting. They contribute to the citizen's ability to follow the law and to accept the responsibilities of citizenship. Skills like attention to detail, searching for information, asking and answering the right questions are essential not only for voting but also complying with government regulations, paying taxes or traveling out of the country as well as using government programs such as the Affordable Care Act, Medicare, Medicaid, and Social Security.

The state of democracy in the United States proves more than ever that general knowledge of the Constitution, federalism, and history of our Republic is not enough. We also need citizens who can think beyond the rhetoric and make intelligent choices in our increasingly complex society.

The Kingdom of Liberal Arts claims that undergraduates become good citizens by studying and discussing major questions covered in the humanities, social sciences, and sciences. It sees knowledge as the path to responsible citizenship. Know-how is rarely ever a focus.

The Kingdom has anointed itself as the main provider of citizenship education, and most people in higher education agree. People buy the Kingdom's conjecture that the life of mind makes good citizens. These people tend to have liberal arts degrees and see themselves as good citizens. They believe the Kingdom's devotion to the sanctity of scholarship and elite preferences can lead to no other conclusion for its members.

Like all deeply held beliefs, the evidence of the role liberal arts education plays in shaping responsible citizens is far from conclusive. That liberal arts graduates predominate in our leadership is a condition of historical fact that older current leaders were more likely to take liberal arts than professional undergraduate degrees, and many political leaders have law degrees which meant that they probably got a liberal arts degree as an undergrad. It is not convincing evidence of cause and effect.

Most of our citizens don't see how the Kingdom contributes to the citizenship of our leaders. As victims of the Kingdom's bait and switch model, they have trouble trusting the institutions providing the education. The Kingdom may encourage discussions of the ideas leading to democracy, but they are using the promise of a fulfilling career to command money and time from students. This cannot be the basis for a healthy relationship between the leaders and the led which is what democracy is supposed to be about.

The fact that attending faculty meetings where the discussions are frequently unpleasant, and consensus is virtually impossible makes one wonder about how liberal arts promotes citizenship. Many faculty and administrators exhibit a commitment to the public good of their institutions, but even more do not. Faculty meetings in the Kingdom are no different than the typical town or school board meetings where the pursuit of special interests and emotions dominate. If undergraduates were to see these meetings, the faculty would not be good role models for them to follow.

A classic document about citizenship is the Athenian Oath which proclaims that citizenship is leaving society better than it was found and exercising rights and responsibilities. Over the past 30 years, the Kingdom has preached to its undergraduates to improve society and to individual rights. The emphasis on the responsibility of a citizen is rarely part of the Kingdom's message. When I ask my class of 100+ students what is an important characteristic of being a good citizen, the response is several different ways of saying "social justice." When I ask, "what else?" the students almost never say "paying taxes" or even "complying with the laws."

The failure of students to appreciate the importance of the responsibilities of citizens is a result of the Kingdom's focus on abstract discussions of citizenship. The focus on knowledge and not know-how is a direct result of the failure of undergraduates to see citizenship as more than making the world better.

The faculty will frequently claim an educated citizenry is crucial for democratic institutions. By "educated," faculty members of the Kingdom mean "knowledgeable" and not necessarily skilled in understanding laws or working toward compromise and the public interest. They assume that having the right ideas will lead to responsible citizenship. Citizenship requires not just the mind but also the heart, which includes emotions, self-interest, and guiding principles, and it requires the tools necessary to make informed decisions.

Developing responsible citizens starts with how students can become responsible citizens while in college. Discussions of what is a good citizen or reading the constitution and why students should vote are not enough. Students need to practice exercising rights and responsibilities while in college, including the classroom. They also need some basic professional skills like using percentages.

Undergraduates can practice behaviors of a responsible citizen by understanding the policies that impact them and expressing their concerns about those policies in a thoughtful way, but they don't. They tend to learn the opposite by not studying the degree requirements and then asking their advisors what the requirements are, by not attending classes with little or no sanctions, and by talking to each other about "unfair" policies or actions rather than talking to faculty and administrators. The faculty, advisors, and administrators sometimes neither listen to their concerns in a systematic way nor correct the students for their lack of compliance and attention to detail. Many faculty do not have much knowledge on liberal arts core requirements and sometimes even the major requirements of their own department, which raises questions about their responsible citizenship.

This lack of knowledge by both leads to poor communication between students and faculty. If more energy were put into understanding requirements by both sides, they would have something they could talk to each other about. This would provide context for them to learn to listen to each other and trust each other and practice responsible citizenship on both sides.

One example of how the Kingdom's faculty tend not to take students seriously is their attitude about student surveys for course feedback. Faculty members frequently become defensive with the result of surveys of the classes they teach. They see the feedback as criticism only rather than signals to think about change. Faculty and administrators take little action to ensure a solid response rate, and therefore show it is a low priority.

The majority of undergraduates view their college as an institution that is untrustworthy. The list provided below is reminiscent of the grievances listed in the Declaration of Independence.

- High tuition and other costs are a form of taxation without representation

- Closed classes because there are not enough seats for those required to take them, and the popular teachers and courses are unavailable
- Degree requirements that are not easily justifiable requiring coursework undergraduates would not choose
- More incentives for the top students than the weaker students
- Inadequate food, housing, and health services
- Inadequate preparation to be on a viable career path once they graduate
- Too much bureaucratic red tape in getting minors or majors, taking courses in different college units of the university, choosing dorm rooms, or help from financial aid

These grievances may or may not be justified, but they exist, are perceived to be ignored by those in authority and breed mistrust of the institution.

Many undergraduates see their college as their government and an authoritarian regime that fails to meet the promises they were given. Whether their expectations are too high or they do not take advantage of the opportunities they were given is beside the point. The distrust of the government they are living under translates into the distrust of all institutions. If trust could be developed for their college, students would practice the tasks of a responsible citizen. They would be responsible in pushing their rights and policies to improve the university. This would help students to trust other institutions including the government. Responsible citizens must appreciate how rules developed by complex institutions can be contradictory, seem to be arbitrary, and require collaboration among people to improve society.

Those who are ruled always have a tendency to question the rulers. It's only natural when they are asked to constrain their freedom and give up their money. The only way the ruled can develop respect for their rulers is if they see their rulers as necessary and ultimately on their side. Responsible citizens can only exist if they appreciate the role of rulers in a complex society.

The well-documented left-wing orientation of the majority of the Kingdom's faculty may raise additional distrust among students for colleges. Many students agree with the views of that orientation, but the constant call for social justice from faculty who are making $100,000+ a year and living the life of an intellectual aristocrat may seem hypocritical to them.

In addition to this very general viewpoint about how the distrust of college may transfer into a lack of commitment to governmental institutions, undergraduates don't acquire the professional skills necessary for their careers that would help them become better citizens.

In 1999, 562 university presidents signed "The Presidents' Declaration on the Civic Responsibility of Higher Education" where they stated, "We share a special concern about the disengagement of college students from democratic participation."[1] While this statement shows that the presidents thought something was wrong, they made the liberal arts and elitist mistake of thinking citizenship was democratic participation. It is a sign of both the feeling that colleges could do more for responsible citizenship among its graduates and thinking that citizenship is only about voting and trust in the political process. At the same time, the Declaration led to the creation of Campus Compact which has a goal of having institutions of higher education support community service which is an important step in the right direction.

One trend in undergraduate education, partially driven by Campus Compact, is that more students are developing a commitment to responsible citizenship through community service, internships, and student activities on campus, instead of their classes. Working for a nonprofit or government agency as an intern or volunteer introduces students to smaller organizations where they can observe the commitment of the employees and take part in the community they create. Student organizations, whether Greek life or others, provide an opportunity to be a responsible member or, if the organization is a mess, help students figure out that the lack of civic commitment to the organization is not something they want to be part of.

THE PATH TO EQUITY AND INCLUSION

The overall point of this discussion is to emphasize that developing citizenship is more about know-how than acquiring abstract or historical knowledge. Know-how is about changing behavior, and behavior can only be changed through experience. Undergraduates need to practice good citizenship if they are going to see that rights and responsibility are part of citizenship.

If the Kingdom were built on a trusted relationship with its undergraduates, then its faculty members would see the students as citizens and would figure out ways to help students act as responsible citizens. They would see that reading and discussing abstractions are not enough. They would understand serving the community, developing the skills to exercise rights and responsibilities, and making intelligent voting choices were more important. Treating citizenship as something to be studied and discussed is not as important as treating it as a way of life at the personal and community level. Treating students as responsible members of the Kingdom's community is critical for a more inclusive experience for our students. The Kingdom could do this by placing students on curriculum committees, encouraging student governments to help improve the college, and giving more credit for community service.

Equity has not been discussed in this chapter; however, it is relevant to the need for students to develop their citizenship skills. In the university, commoners could have leadership roles in shaping university policies to make sure their interests are served. With that experience, the students would have a path to becoming influential in their communities so that they can get their interests served.

NOTE

1. *Presidents' Declaration on the Civic Responsibility of Higher Education | Campus Compact.* 23 Mar. 2009, https://compact.org/resources/presidents-declaration-on-the-civic-responsibility-of-higher-education.

Chapter 17

Too Many Thinkers; Not Enough Doers

> Thinking is easy, acting is difficult, and to put one's thoughts into action is the most difficult thing in the world.
>
> —Johann Wolfgang von Goethe

America has too many market researchers and not enough salespeople, too many education policy analysts and a shortage of teachers, too many people studying poverty and not enough mentors and caseworkers in the trenches, too many human resources staff and not enough managers who act to improve employees through coaching and, if necessary, firing. The decline of doers has created serious shortages in many professional fields like nursing, medicine, teaching, social work, plumbing, and policing.

While the Kingdom produces too many thinkers and not enough doers through its undergraduate education, the damage is much more extensive for American society as mentioned in Chapter 15, K–12 Toxicity. One only has to read reports and newspaper accounts of the shortages in America for unskilled and skilled workers. Or maybe, the reader has found it hard to hire a plumber.

K–12 students and their parents are socialized to believe that the only path to wealth and happiness is through college. The many paths for the 65% of American adults aged 25 years and above who don't have college degrees proves that a college degree is not the only path to economic security.

Social work students who came to college with dreams of working directly with clients change their goals while in college. Students who were thinking about a career in improving K–12 education don't want to become teachers even initially. They want to study education so they can fix it without any experience. Pre-meds give up their dreams of becoming a doctor when they run into organic chemistry. Most college students don't consider sales because they feel that it is beneath them. Many students who aim for law school do not necessarily want to become practicing lawyers to take care of clients. They see law school as a way to think like a lawyer, whatever that means. Too many law school graduates can't pass the bar, so they can't be doers in their chosen profession.

This mismatch between higher education and workforce needs is a result of many factors other than the role of the Kingdom. The most important is that the growing complexity of society and the advances in technology require more creative problem-solving by decision makers who need more information. Massive amounts of data are accumulating to help decision-makers make the "right" decision.

Decision-makers are searching for thinkers to help them assess both risks and opportunities by getting solid and relevant background analysis, looking for models to make forecasts of alternative scenarios, and evaluating the results of decisions. The analysts are in effect personal advisors to the decision-makers and more likely to receive higher salaries than the individuals providing direct services and products. Whether or not the analysts really help the decision-makers will be discussed later in this chapter. The point here is that decision-makers are driving the growth in thinkers through higher salaries.

One clear example of the high value placed on data analysis by decision-makers is the increased role of data analytic workers in the field of sports like baseball. They spend millions of dollars on data analytics in order to get to and win the World Series proves the point.

Data analysis can inform decision-makers by providing probabilities of the conditions in the future or the impact of policy decisions. The decision makers still have to make the decisions. The Kingdom teaches its graduates the more information the better because of its commitment to scholarship. Decision-makers believe the more information the better not just to make the right decision but to reduce criticisms. This has created a massive demand for information and for staff to collect, organize, and analyze the information which may or may not be worth the cost, but which generates a demand for thinkers.

College students have benefited from this demand for thinkers because they think the benefits outweigh the cost of the analyst jobs when compared to the doer jobs. Thinkers get paid more and don't have to deal with the messiness of working directly with clients or physical operations. The idea of working with one's hands, being subject to the demands of customers, or being told what to do by management is not as appealing as putting together a written or oral briefing with the help of a couple of colleagues. In addition, advising decision makers is almost like being in the elite and therefore more likely to help them move up in their careers.

Higher education in general has created conditions for thinkers rather than a culture for doers. Undergraduates spend four years as a child trying to become an adult. Freedom may be the most important feature of their existence. They don't have to attend the majority of classes and are not spending much time outside of class studying. Enjoying freedom and talking to each other and faculty about ideas is what they think they are going to do when they get a job in the real world. As a result, they are trained to avoid the mundane and the repetitive, which is what doers do.

I had a student who was doing well in college both academically and socially. He got a full semester internship working at a high school in New York City and had to get up at 6:00 a.m. to get to the school by 8:00 a.m. and frequently did not come home until 8:00 p.m. After two weeks, he wouldn't get out of bed in his apartment, and his mother had to come get him to take him home. This is an extreme example of why college life is like a day on the beach or a four-year summer camp, at a very high financial cost, compared to having a 9 to 5 doer job. As a result of this experience, he decided to pursue an analyst job.

Thinkers are great at making jobs for themselves. They convince government and private foundations to subsidize their speculation. Big business, despite its claims that it is more efficient than the other two sectors, is not immune to this pressure. The revolution in technology has increased access to information that leads all decision-makers to hire more people to find the needle in the haystack and give them an edge. Once people are hired, they lobby for more analysts by claiming the workload is too great, and it is better to have more opinions than fewer opinions.

While these factors have played a major role in the shortage of doers and the abundance of thinkers, the Kingdom has contributed to the condition. Being mostly liberal arts graduates themselves, managers like to have people who are interested in what they are interested in. People bring the culture of their college into their career worlds and generally use feeling comfortable as a measure of trust.

Their education path from kindergarten to college graduation which is shaped by the Kingdom provides little opportunity for students who want to deliver direct services. The stigma attached to "vocational programs" reinforces the incentive of more money in those jobs that play with data rather than deliver products or services or manage those who deliver them.

With a background in academic research, the new job holders are considered qualified to do applied research. How useful their research is is rarely questioned because decision-makers believe the more research the better just like members of the Kingdom believe the more formal education the better. Liberal arts scholarship may not prepare graduates for applied research since the scholarship is heavy on abstractions and theories.

The Kingdom has been a prime factor in pushing the market for thinkers. They use the term "critical thinkers" to justify their focus on scholarly research which is quite different in each discipline. Leaders, most of whom graduated from liberal arts programs, think the Kingdom produces the best analysts. Whether the leaders are right or wrong is not important. What's important is that the salaries of the analysts and the demand for more analysts goes up.

Having the BA and then maybe a graduate degree in a professional school means higher costs to the organization to pay for the people providing the analysis. The huge investment in data analysis keeps millions of workers busy at a relatively high salary. The jobs almost always require a college degree, more often than not in the liberal arts, and they encourage more graduate training which requires a BA or BS to enter graduate school in most cases.

As discussed in Chapter 12, The Anxiety Machine, the Kingdom promotes optionitis because the emphasis is on breadth not depth. The students are faced with a buffet of ideas, cultures, theories, and tools. They have trouble making a commitment to focus on some area which might prepare them to eventually do something, especially if they can connect to an internship experience outside of academia. The students have trouble finding such real-world experiences and instead are offered research positions by lobby groups, political groups, and nonprofits. Having no real-world experience, they flit from one field to another.

Part of the liberal arts folkway fed to undergraduates is that they should pursue their interests. With little real-world experience and the naive idea that what is taught in the Kingdom's course provides a meaningful experience on what they are interested in, they keep looking for the right subject. Even if they found a major that interests them, they would have little idea of what people do in the field and are therefore unable to make a choice. So, they end up thinking, for example, that what is studied in international relations classes is what they would do in the U.S. Department of State. Why would they know how naive that view is?

Students are introduced to thinker careers through coursework which the Kingdom and the professional schools offer. Even if they want to be salespersons, for example, they will take a course in marketing if they are in a business school. They will study theories of marketing rather than the people skills needed to be a successful salesperson. If they are in a liberal arts program, they will not be introduced to sales programs.

They will be discouraged for ideological reasons because the Kingdom's faculty don't want their students to go into what they see as the selfish role of "businessperson." They want their students to fix the world so they can feel good about undergraduate teaching. They will also remind students that they didn't go to college to do sales. Despite the enormous demands for salespeople and the potential to make large amounts of money, the students would prefer to do market research or public relations.

Students don't understand that market research and public relations are in effect thinkers to help salespeople make sales. They may be on the number cruncher or creative side which they have been conditioned to think are fun. They don't realize that salespeople who work on commission can make more money than market researchers if they have the right product. They also don't realize that the number of sales is a direct measure of performance while no measures exist for ideas and analysis other than what their boss thinks.

Despite the investment in analysts, many leaders have trouble getting the answers they need. The analysts themselves have trouble understanding what the leaders want because the analysts are thinking more about explanations than predictions. Harry Truman searched for a one-armed economist because he was tired of hearing "on the one hand and on the other hand" from them. Failing to get what they want, decision-makers hire more analysts while they keep the old ones.

A colleague and I conducted a study for the U.S. Department of State which revealed that the decision-makers at the under-secretary of state level and above were dissatisfied with the work of intelligent analysts in the department. Decision-makers want clear predictions, but the analysts want to provide interesting explanations. In addition, the researchers themselves like to show how knowledgeable they are rather than give clear understandable advice to busy decision makers on what they think will happen or the consequences of different policies. State Department and CIA analysts reminded me of professors generating speculation for its own sake.

The pernicious effect of the focus on thinking rather than doing can be seen in the behavior of leaders at all levels where more time is spent on creating policies and less time is spent on making sure the policies are executed. It is inherent in the nature of things that the bigger the institutions, the poorer the execution because there are so many moving parts.

The tendency for all institutions to deliberate forever but then to fail to anticipate unintended consequences. They also tend to not provide enough financial and staff resources to execute the policy well. They prefer to debate policy more than do the hard work necessary to implement it. Two major policy initiatives illustrate the point.

The No Child Left Behind Act was an attempt to raise standards and create more uniformity in educational standards across socio-economic classes and geographical areas. It ignored the overwhelming differences in a country as big and diverse as the United States. It ignored what the people in the trenches, aka teachers, were saying, not to mention the students who were dismissed as whiners. The primary beneficiaries of No Child Left Behind were the consultants and the travel and entertainment sectors that hosted conferences. The concept of using metrics to drive change was hopelessly naive from the outside, something the Kingdom encourages with its cultivation of idealism over realism and its failure to accept that representative and valid data is rare.

The policies to reduce trade barriers were based on theories supporting free trade and the idea of globalism. It received bipartisan support because it appealed to abstractions on both the right and the left. While those who lost their jobs opposed these movements, the impacted community leaders rarely voiced objections and sat idly by as the rust belt communities and workers were economically devastated. Some opposition developed, but it did not lead to the increase in the power of unions or adjustment to ameliorate the negative effects on workers. Instead, the opposition like Occupy Wall Street which had many protests and became more prominent in the media voiced socialist and Marxists rhetoric. Abstract thinking led to globalist economic policies and the only response that made the media was more abstract exchanges about capitalism versus socialism.

America needs people who will do something rather than speculate and discuss in order to reach a decision. It is not clear if the need for doers will be met. College in general and the Kingdom have helped create this condition, but employers and the current generation have made matters worse.

THE PATH TO EQUITY AND INCLUSION

The most important way the Kingdom can help college graduates take jobs that produce something other than analysis is to create more experiential learning. Students need to learn about the large variety of jobs by working with troops on the ground whether it is in sales, management, social work, election campaigning, advertising, customer service, or delivering programs to clients for governmental and nonprofit agencies. Internship, community service, and hands-on projects for teams and individuals will give students exposure to careers and having a boss as discussed in Chapter 14.

Experiences outside of academics require students to do mundane things where there are immediate positive results. Once they work in community service or internships or even projects that require dealing with outside clients, their fear of doing mundane things may dissipate. They may learn to love these tasks because when a job is finished, there is a feeling of accomplishment based on something concrete.

The Kingdom has to provide better and more realistic research experiences. The traditional theoretical research of the social sciences and the textual analysis of the humanities along with highly technical research of the physical science are all different from the problem-solving framework which relies more on predictions and evaluations than theoretical explanations tested by data or logic and confirmed by the professor. These experiences will be powerful in shaping undergraduates' paths to becoming professional adults. It will also give them a sense of accomplishment that may encourage them to do work that requires more than academic skills and to enter careers that at least start with doing rather than just thinking analytically.

Working in an internship or job will introduce undergraduates to the importance of management in the functioning of organizations. Management in any organization is the path to higher wages and more challenging conditions. Starting in a mundane and grinding job will lead to opportunities for management, and students will see that. They will also see that the skills that they are supposed to learn from the Kingdom are about problem-solving and therefore thinking. But it will be thinking from the perspective of a doer.

The fact that liberal arts push students into thinkers' jobs is a barrier to equity and inclusion. This advantages the better prepared students and disadvantages the commoners who do not love learning for its own sake and abstractions. Since most doer jobs (except for sales) lead to lower salaries than thinker jobs, equity is not served. People hiring for thinker jobs are in a different culture than those who may not be excelling in liberal arts academics. They are likely to say something like, "she's not an analyst," which is code for, "I can't see her being in my tribe."

If equity and inclusion are to be improved by the work of the Kingdom, faculty could emphasize the opportunities for economic success that comes from sales and other doer jobs. In addition, the Kingdom's faculty could encourage students to take minors in professional fields like management, information studies, and visual and performing arts. They could also encourage students to look for internships where they would be doers rather than research assistants.

Chapter 18

Equity Denied

> The basic task of leadership is to increase the standard of living and the quality of life for all stakeholders.
>
> —Stephen R. Covey

Higher Education may help some poor and middle class people move up the income ladder, but its overall impact on society is to make the rich and upper middle class richer and the rest poorer. Soaring tuition costs has transferred wealth to institutions of higher education from the pocketbooks of middle and poor America. The rich suffer little from the college tuition "tax." It is a drop in the bucket for the rich and not likely to change their standard of living. For the poor and middle class, the impact on their income and wealth is enormous. Those families have had to take on second jobs, second mortgages, deplete their wealth, and take on debt that lasts for some into their sixties. In the meantime, the universities have been able to gain funds from alumni to support research and athletic programs more than undergraduate education.

The Kingdom keeps the pressure up in K–12 education to push students away from the kinds of know-how they need for employment with or without college as discussed in Chapters 15 and 17. The Kingdom's own research suggests that college is a path to social mobility, but other studies like *Born to Win, Schooled to Lose* suggest otherwise.[1] The burden of the anti-careerist pressures in K–12 and college education fall especially on the poor.

High school students are required, sometimes by state graduation exams, to learn Algebra 2 and demonstrate an understanding of both an infinite variety of subjects ranging from the science of chemistry to English literature. These requirements give additional power to the Kingdom to improve the life of the mind rather than to help students gain the know-how they need to succeed in whatever they want to succeed in.

Equity is damaged by a K–12 curriculum based on the Kingdom's commitment to the life of the mind because it does not serve students who do not go to college. Despite the needs-based discounts and the many great stories of the relatively few who get to the American Dream after college, equity is not served for the majority. The Kingdom likes to publicize the need-based funding and the feel-good stories, but one wonders how many feel-bad stories are out there. Could the odds be 100 feel-bad to 1 feel-good stories?

For college students, the statistics on college completion and debt demonstrate the opposite of equity. About 60% of college students graduate in six years, a rate as bad as the lowest performing high school.[2] Over 60% of college students graduate with debt averaging more than $30,000.[3] Sixty percent of students from the lowest 20% of income attend college[4] while 20% from that same stratum graduate college.[5]

Increasing accessibility to college without a commensurate increase in graduation rate is the opposite of equity. Students who attend and don't graduate not only wasted their time and money, but also may have increased their debt and suffered the stigma of dropout. Even if they eventually graduate, they may have problems getting jobs worth the time and money that led to their degree. Based on the gap between the percent of poor attending college and the percent who graduate, higher education does more harm than good to the disadvantaged.

These statements are true of college in general, but the Kingdom of Liberal Arts plays a large role not only in failing to promote equity and inclusion, but in doing the opposite. The commitment to the sanctity of scholarship gives specific advantages to the well-prepared students and creates significant barriers for the poorly prepared students.

The Kingdom's bait and switch business model leads most commoners to think that they will be gaining the know-how they need to succeed. As noted in Chapter 12, the better prepared students who come from more educated and wealthy parents and high schools steeped in the liberal arts know that the liberal arts are far from career preparation. They have been socialized to play the game, and most will do so. They have the background to help them prepare for careers while they pursue learning for its own sake. They know how important it is to get internships and experiences and their parents' rich friends help them get there.

Whether that background comes from their parents or the network of friends who have gone to college and ended up well, the better prepared students know the drill. The poorly prepared students don't have the background to realize that scholarship is the goal of liberal arts program and don't know how to pursue the skills to supplement their liberal arts education. It takes them years to figure out how to benefit from the college experience.

Meanwhile, the undergraduate professional schools have more rigorous standards for admission, so they are less likely to admit poorly prepared students. As a result, those students have no choice but to take and stay in liberal arts. They must continue to be judged by standards of scholarship.

The Kingdom's influence not only reaches through the K–12 system, as already discussed. It also heavily influences community and junior colleges. These two-year colleges offer many vocationally oriented subjects like auto mechanics, X-ray technicians, and criminal justice, but the liberal arts faculty in community colleges demand a piece of the pie.

The major sales pitch by too many community colleges is that it is a cheaper way of getting a four-year degree. This is a reasonable sales pitch except that it ignores the bait and switch business model of the Kingdom. Community college students are more likely than four-year college students to be commoners, which means that they are not aware that the four-year liberal arts degree is about scholarship rather than career preparation.

I know many students who have benefited cost-wise by community colleges, and I know many who have not. Even if they finish the four-year program, it is usually in liberal arts. If they don't graduate, they spend two years not developing professional skills because they were taking liberal arts coursework. The sales pitch to save money for a four-year degree is more attractive than getting a specific job skill like HVAC. The Kingdom rules through its proxy of two-year colleges.

The marketing of community colleges as a way to save money on college ignores the fact that 60% of students in community college take remedial courses.[6] Remedial courses do not generate college credit but do generate tuition bills. In some cases, the students use any scholarship fund available or go into debt to pay for remedial credits that do not go to degree requirements. The community colleges are viewed as a path to equity when for some it is a path to remaining poor.

I had a high school mentee who was poor and had some disabilities. He could not pass the New York State regents exams. After joining the Job Core and completing the program successfully, he joined the military where he was the top recruit in his class. After an honorable discharge, he wanted to be a policeman, so he was advised to go to community college.

He called me one night and told me the trouble he was having with the coursework. Then he asked me why he needed to learn both APA and MLA citation systems. He said, "can't they make up their mind?" The APA-MLA battle is just one of many esoteric challenges the Kingdom imposes on students. He never made it through community college but did all right for himself working union jobs and benefiting from a military pension. He had the will to overcome all that the educational system threw at him.

The Kingdom's war against equity starts right in the freshman year when the students from better backgrounds are likely to benefit from the many college credits earned in high school through AP courses, the International

Baccalaureate Program, or concurrent enrollment programs. This means that these students can avoid many of the liberal arts core courses and go right into studying what they are interested in. Lower division liberal arts courses may be more difficult than upper division courses. This creates an easier road for the better prepared students. The most important factor is that the better students have more choices than the commoners. They can focus on their interests sooner than the students with poorer backgrounds.

Better prepared students spend money on both AP and SAT tutoring because they tend to come from wealth. Students who don't have these resources may not be able to get a 4 on an AP test or raise their SAT scores. In the long run, that will result in less merit scholarship money and fewer college credits coming into college for the poorly prepared students.

Watching their roommates get out of liberal arts core requirements while not being able to take classes in their specific interests, the poorly prepared students suffered more from the anxiety the Kingdom creates discussed in Chapter 12. They also are reminded yet again of the advantages that come to students from wealthy and highly educated parents. Lower division liberal arts core requirements could be viewed as a form of forced remediation on students to make up for poor liberal arts courses in high school, but in reality, it operates as a barrier to the poorly prepared students that some of them cannot get past.

Universities try to offset the disadvantages of the poorly prepared students through programs like the Higher Education Opportunity Program (HEOP), a federally funded program for students from low-income families that are not well-prepared. They may also offer summer school courses before the first semester to give the students a head-start as well as six or so credits that generate higher GPAs. This may help reduce the gap for a small number of poorly prepared students but not for the vast majority of commoners who come from lower middle class and poor families.

Universities, especially those in the Kingdom, keep rewarding the better students with awards, tuition grants if they have above a certain GPA level, and money for summer internships and research projects. The honors programs are designed to attract and keep the better prepared students through these kinds of incentives. The sanctity of scholarship drives most of these awards and does not help poorly prepared students. They are not driven by the desire to learn for the sake of learning and are therefore less likely to do as well academically.

To add to the inequity in the system, bringing in 20–30 college credits from high schools means that the student can graduate in three years rather than four. Saving 25% of tuition and living costs and getting into the job market a year early benefits the better students. The 25% bonus goes to those who need it less.

The vast majority of the Kingdom's faculty members support these enhancements to reward the better prepared students even as they say they advocate equity and inclusion. The Kingdom talks about DEI by forming committees, making administrative appointments, and generating public relations "proving" a commitment to equity. However, as long as the Kingdom's focus remains on scholarship, it will create disadvantages for the students who need the most help in preparing for careers.

The role of the Kingdom in the selective promotion of DEI is the result of its narrow focus on the life of the mind. The DEI treatments have been directed at changing the attitude of administrators, faculty members, and students. It takes the form of interpreting history, discussion sessions in person or online, and the establishment of operational policies in areas like public relations, hiring, freshman training sessions, and required faculty and staff training.

The commoners who come to college from the middle and lower classes are ignored as an identifiable group because they represent the majority of undergraduates. The poorly prepared students cannot be easily organized as readily as the interest groups who represent specific identities or minority groups. The Kingdom's bait and switch business model disadvantages the commoners most regardless of their ethnic, gender, or other backgrounds around which they are organized.

It is as if the Kingdom's DEI supporters believe that undergraduates' behavior towards others will be more inclusive through academic discussions. Its members ignore the reality that students are increasingly disengaged from academic pursuits. The Kingdom's faculty either don't realize or pretend not to realize that undergraduate behaviors are shaped by personal experience and the cultural environment they grew up in. The most effective way to change people's basic attitudes is to have them work with people from different socioeconomic and racial backgrounds. Reading academic literature will not shape the behavior of the majority of students in college.

Looking at the entire college experience of undergraduates, courses play a minor role compared to living in the residence hall, student activities, and community experiences, not to mention their family and community background. Working with a diverse crew at Dunkin Donuts may have a more powerful impact than reading and discussing diversity literature. As a result of increased student and parental pressure, there has been a gradual movement to experience credit and community service over the past two decades by the Kingdom which is a step in the right direction and may have had a greater effect than diversity training. It would have been even more powerful if the Kingdom's faculty could see community service either as a volunteer or for credit as essential to the goal of DEI.

Despite the movement towards community service, the emphasis on the literature of diversity seems to be the strategy of choice. At Syracuse, several students who were peer instructors in a one credit freshman course covering DEI told me that they suggested to the leaders of the course that the readings were too much and too academic but to no avail. Some community activities are included in some of the sections, but it is not uniform or central enough. Under the theme of diversity, a group might visit an art museum as a community experience. The Kingdom appears to think that putting commoners in an art museum will result in enlightenment. The Kingdom's faculty may have this view because they found such visits useful to themselves.

A legitimate research question raised by the DEI movement is whether or not the assumption that promoting specific ideas through discussions and readings leads to changed behavior. The idea that announcements and training from above without being backed up by laws and sanctions is what life of the mind devotees think changes behaviors. The Kingdom's faculty are true believers who act as if liberal arts is a religion and that sermons and responsive readings can change behaviors. Most religions have the same problem in changing behavior for the same reason. Only each individual can make the change as a result of life experiences.

Another example of equity denied is that faculty searches do not value candidates who have online PhDs. Many African American applicants and applicants from poor backgrounds obtain their PhDs through online programs. When it comes to inviting people into their elite world, the Kingdom's faculty cannot imagine that online degrees would produce PhD candidates who are as excellent as they are in research.

Ignoring the tension between merit and equity is the most important problem in the deliberations generated by DEI because it ignores the powerful influence of the class division in society and in colleges. The commoners who attend college are faced with a separation between their goal of preparing for careers after college and the educational goals of the Kingdom to make students better scholars. While the Kingdom proclaims dedication to equity, the concern over the standards of scholarship creates barriers.

The liberal arts faculties' commitment to scholarship above all and their training as scholars stand in the way of diversity, equity, and inclusion. The idea of merit is essential to the training of scholars; yet merit gets in the way of changes in hiring, curriculum, and student evaluations. Rather than recognize the tension between equity and merit, some pretend there are no tensions while others take an either-or position. Some think that embracing equity will let the barbarians into their city while others think that equity is the only right thing to do. These are deep seated attitudes that cannot change if not discussed openly.

The merit-equity conflict is not discussed openly because it is too hot to keep it from exploding into emotional exchanges that reveal that the Kingdom cannot remain rational. It would conflict with the Kingdom's view that liberal arts is the home of the intellectuals who see truth through free speech. As long as it remains the invisible elephant in the room, the kinds of pragmatic and incremental steps that would lead to reasonable changes cannot be met.

The Kingdom has contributed to what Will Bunch said in his book, *After the Ivory Tower Falls: How College Broke the American Dream and Blew Up Our Politics and How to Fix It*, the class warfare between the "non-college crowd" and their "diploma bearing foes." The election of Donald Trump in 2016 made clear that class warfare between the commoners and the elites was real. The overall effect has been to create a stalemate and to slow down substantive reforms that could lead to more social mobility than that which exists now.

THE PATH TO EQUITY AND INCLUSION

The Kingdom needs to reset its treatment of equity by recognizing the tensions between equity and merit. The merit defenders are bullied by the equity supporters today after hundreds of years of bullying the defenders of equity. The influx of commoners into undergraduate education starting with the policies at the end of World War II designed to find a place for millions of returning veterans was done out of fear that they would take to the streets as well as appreciation for the sacrifices those veterans made. The pre–World War II model was driven by merit, but the post–WWII model was driven by the fact that there were millions of commoners who were promised an education as part of a workforce policy.

The Kingdom of Liberal Arts has played a central role in generating tensions between undergraduates and faculty as well as between the university and the government which could have been easily resolved if it combined workforce preparation with preparation for life and citizenship. This would require compromises by the Kingdom to allow more credit for undergraduate professional development while also reducing the focus on scholarship as an end in itself. It should have provided coursework that starts where most commoners are, especially at the lower division level. The Kingdom's faculty should have continued their research work, perhaps with a slightly lower priority, to set policies and adapt some courses to meet the goals of careers and citizenship.

Despite the past failure, the Kingdom's faculty can still learn that balancing the life of the mind with life is important and will not be the death of liberal art. The bait and switch business model has created a system that denies equity and inclusion. The fix is to provide more academic credit for experiential learning, Social Emotional Learning and professional development. Commoners will respond well if the Kingdom can reduce the number of credits in which the pursuit of scholarship is the primary goal.

NOTES

1. "Born to Win, Schooled to Lose: Why Equally Talented Students Don't Get Equal Chances to Be All They Can Be." *CEW Georgetown*, https://cew.georgetown.edu/cew-reports/schooled2lose/. Accessed 28 Jan. 2023.

2. *Shocking Statistics About College Graduation Rates*. https://www.forbes.com/sites/markkantrowitz/2021/11/18/shocking-statistics-about-college-graduation-rates/?sh=38d06dec2b69. Accessed 28 Jan. 2023.

3. *Student Loans and the Cancellation Debate, Part 1 by NerdWallet's Smart Money Podcast.player.megaphone.fm*, https://player-origin.megaphone.fm/NRD8164832452. Accessed 28 Jan. 2023.

4. Center, NSC Research. "High School Benchmarks—2019." *National Student Clearinghouse Research Center*, 7 Oct. 2019, https://nscresearchcenter.org/high-school-benchmarks-2019/.

5. *Immediate College Enrollment Rate*, 2000.

6. *Why Do 60% of Community College Students Need Remedial Coursework?* https://www.communitycollegereview.com/blog/why-do-60-of-community-college-students-need-remedial-coursework. Accessed 28 Jan. 2023.

PART V

Foundational Changes for Equity and Inclusion

How three key changes could lead to a transformation just underway.

Chapter 19

Change PhD Education

> Will any one pretend for a moment that the doctor's degree is a guarantee that its possessor will be successful as a teacher?
>
> —William James, 1903

The Kingdom's academic tribes are insular when it comes to undergraduate education. The faculty see students as something to be transformed from uneducated to educated. Faculty view undergraduates as outsiders who have difficulty connecting with them. The few students they connect with become recruits for eventual tribal membership. Like most tribes, the outside world is to be converted or ignored.

The Kingdom's faculty members also see administrators as outsiders. Even though the administrators usually come from the faculty, their need to respond to customers, Boards of Trustees, and the community makes them less insular than the faculty. As a result, the faculty are suspicious of administrators. Faculty members frequently use the term "going to the dark side" when colleagues become administrators.

The tribal behavior is a result of socialization, "the process of learning to behave in a way that is acceptable to society."[1] PhD training is a socialization process that produces this insularity. Tribalism creates an extraordinary commitment to scholarship in general and the disciplinary tribe in particular. It suggests that providing what students need and pay for is secondary to the Kingdom.

Devotion to the idea of the scholar is the purpose of the PhD training that includes taking courses, working closely with a few faculty, completing assistantship activities, taking comprehensive exams, writing a dissertation, as well as commiserating with other graduate students and going to faculty events. The capstone of the socialization process is writing and defending the PhD dissertation which can be stressful and take years. This can only be viewed as a long and painful form of socialization. After four to eight years of training, the successful PhD candidates become citizens of the Kingdom driven to continue the Kingdom.

The PhD is essential for the faculty members' feeling of self-worth. Devoted to scholarship as the essence of their profession, they spend most of their time in scholarly research and in teaching activities to find and nurture future scholars. Faculty see that scholarly activity is inherently valuable, and the major purpose of a liberal arts education.

The path through which faculty members go to obtain their PhDs creates allegiance that makes it difficult for faculty to consider all but a few of their students as outsiders. Faculty want their students to desire to study their scholarly fields. When they see resistance from most students, they find it difficult to enjoy teaching their students. This tension is the source of frustration for both professors and undergraduates. They are at cross-purposes which creates mutual distrust, the root cause of the lack of equity and inclusion in undergraduate education.

The communication gap between professor and commoner is assumed not to be as great by the faculty as it is. Confronted with this communication gap, professors frequently come to the conclusion that the students are not very bright. Faculty members are often heard saying to each other and administrators, "I would not continue teaching undergraduates if it were not for a few of my students who are brilliant." Brilliant means participating in the same scholarly activities as the professor. Their lectures and treatment of students are designed to find brilliant students who the faculty can enjoy, not nearly the goal of inclusiveness.

As discussed in Chapter 8, the desire of the faculty to be called "professors" suggests that the instructors are the superior authority, and the students are receivers of wisdom. The term itself is the source of the poor relationship between the commoners and the faculty. At the very least, the relationship should be the professor as service provider and the student as client. Faculty don't see students as customers on the grounds that the students have to learn and, if they don't, it's their fault. Students see themselves as customers who want to get what they are paying for. The conflict over their respective roles must change if the trust between undergraduates and faculty is to grow.

Even though the tasks of the faculty are described as research, teaching, and service, scholarly research dominates PhD training while teaching is secondary and service is tertiary. PhD training generates such a deep commitment to scholarship that shapes the behavior of the Kingdom's faculty and the Kingdom's policies.

College graduates who choose to obtain PhDs face four to eight years of training in the latest research, culture, and language of the tribe. The prolonged and constant socialization creates true believers in the value of scholarship and the superiority of their tribe. PhD candidates who don't conform to the folkways of the tribe don't get their PhDs. Those who conform do.

The socialization continues if the new PhDs stay in academia either as a tenure track professor, a teaching professor, or a postdoc or adjunct. If they are tenure track, they have to publish extensively in peer review articles and obtain tenure by their seventh year. They are "mentored" which is a continuation of the socialization process, and they are considered a provisional member of the tribe. If they are teaching professors, they are still held to some form of research requirements. If they are in some kind of post-doctoral or visiting position, they are subject to the socialization process required by their search for a job. This means that the socialization process continues long after the PhD is earned.

Faculty want to preserve the sanctity of scholarship above all else. They are inherently conservative when it comes to curriculum and the treatment of both undergraduate and graduate students. After investing four to eight years in the culture of scholarship, they see themselves as preserving folkways they learned to accept. This conservatism towards undergraduates contrasts with the desire of most faculty to change society, their institution, or their own discipline. When it comes to undergraduates, faculty want to treat them as they were treated, vassals of the Kingdom.

The most significant example of the sanctity of scholarship above all else is the overproduction of PhDs. Higher education has a long history of preparing too many PhDs for too few academic jobs. Professors who teach undergraduates find meaning and happiness in encouraging those students that show scholarly traits to become professors. Consequently, PhD programs have been overpopulated for more than half a century. According to the National Science Foundation, "60% of [all] PhDs end up unemployed or in low-paying postdoc positions."[2]

Rather than reduce the number of PhD students, the Kingdom created positions for "postdocs" which gives PhDs who are not able to get permanent faculty positions a job at a lower salary to continue their research and take up some necessary teaching duties. These positions also allow existing faculty to avoid teaching lower division courses so they can do more research and enjoy the pleasure of working with the scholarly students. Rather than reducing the supply of PhDs, the Kingdom has generated lower paying and more risky jobs for their PhDs to offset the decline in full-time positions.

The continuation of the Kingdom's bait and switch business model is used in recruiting PhD students. Graduate students may think at the outset that they are going to become professors whose main job is teaching. They learn that their main job is to publish their scholarly research. When they realize the bait and switch, some PhD candidates will drop out. Despite mounting criticism of the business model and the economic consequences in terms of losing students to professional schools, the Kingdom only takes small steps, rarely within the formal doctoral curriculum, to prepare students as teachers of lower division undergraduates or help them develop the commitment and capacity to serve their department, university, or the community.

The attempt to move PhD training to job preparation outside of academia and research institutes is an example of the general propensity of degree inflation. The primary argument would be that people with PhDs are more skilled in critical thinking and research methods. The trouble with this viewpoint is that critical thinking and methods of research are the same goals of the Kingdom's undergraduate education. For example, if one applicant had a master's in say, chemical engineering, and another had a PhD, the employer would select the PhD unless it cost them a lot more because it is assumed they are better critical thinkers. The argument only has value in the job market if a higher degree creates a more valuable worker.

In recent years, faculty have been encouraged to publish for readers outside of their tribe, including newspapers as well as government, businesses, and nonprofit organizations. Except for newspaper publications, the audiences are specialized to the extent that they are in their own tribes. This has increased some relevance of the faculty's research for upper division undergraduates. However, it may not be relevant to lower division undergraduates who are not focused on specialized subject matter.

Moreover, publication to non-academic sources may not help faculty gain tenure or promotion. The Kingdom's faculty values peer reviewed publications in making personnel decisions. This may vary by type and research prestige of the institution. Peer reviewed articles are rarely understood by the majority of undergraduates. In some cases, peer reviewed articles may not be understood by a sub-tribe within the discipline. For example, the tribe of microeconomists may not understand behavioral economics or vice versa. Insularity of the Kingdom's faculty has no limits. The Kingdom's hiring process promotes the life of the mind and therefore promotes insularity and the divide between undergraduates and faculty.

In the 1970s and 1980s, articles were published in printed journals. This kept the number of scholarly publications fairly low despite the modest increase of new journals as academic sub-tribes multiplied. However, with the onset of online journals, the availability of online peer review journals exploded. The overall effect of this was to put more pressure on faculty to do academic research in their drive for tenure, promotion and high salaries. The list of publications on the resumes of jobseekers has increased. Between peer review and non-peer review publications, faculty have less time to pay attention to their undergraduates.

The growth of professional master's programs represents an attempt by the Kingdom to capture more students by promising career preparation. These programs are subject to the same tensions inherent in the bait and switch business model for undergraduate and PhD students. Those dedicated to their academic discipline and theory lead to conflict with those committed to preparing graduates for a specific set of careers outside of academia and research. Most professional school programs hire a significant number of professors of practice and adjuncts from the fields their students plan to enter to help take care of the career promise. Students who graduate from these programs are satisfied because their main purpose is to get the degree. While they feel many courses are too theoretical to be useful, they see that some of the courses provided them the tools they need. If the students get a job, they may carry resentment towards that part of the master's program that appeared to be too theoretical and abstract, but their purpose was achieved when they got a job.

Another major indicator of the commitment to scholarship above all else is the failure of PhD programs to give a high enough priority to teaching undergraduates. The amount of time and effort given to prepare effective college instructors is minuscule compared to the time spent providing research experience to PhD candidates. Over the past four decades, programs and even credentials in teaching have become add-ons to the existing coursework, comprehensive examinations, and writing dissertations but not integrated into formal course requirements that would reduce the amount of time spent on learning the trade of scholarship. Performance criteria in teaching are not part of whether or not candidates get their PhD. If faculty were to want teaching to be part of the formal curriculum, they would demand that more credits be added on to the PhD or the number of credits based on research be reduced. They would also spend more of their time working with their candidates as teaching apprentices rather than occasional training sessions.

Although professional schools are in the PhD production business, the main engine for too many PhDs is the Kingdom. The Kingdom's faculty see doctoral candidates who have successful research records as a primary measure of their success. Professional school faculty have an obligation to help prepare their students for careers outside academic and research organizations, so the research tends to be more applied than in the Kingdom. However, because the Kingdom is the mothership that gave birth to professional school faculty, the professional school faculty with PhDs follow the path of the Kingdoms as they fight for power and more resources in universities.

Usually, the need to write a dissertation that contributes to knowledge in the candidate's discipline becomes a barrier to obtaining their PhD. The barrier is the result of the viewpoint that their dissertation must contribute new knowledge in the discipline. In the physical sciences, the viewpoint makes some sense, but in the social sciences and humanities, the idea that everything is a footnote to Plato holds some water. The humanities would probably accept this. Scholars in the social sciences, who have tried to ape the physical sciences to gain credibility, would disagree. The commonly used rationale for a dissertation, that it contributes to knowledge in the field and is cumulative, creates an impossible barrier to the dissertation writer if it is strictly interpreted. As a result, it is part of the folkway that increases the commitment to research since it is similar to the search for the Holy Grail.

A more important barrier is the hesitation of dissertation advisors in deciding if the dissertation is good enough. This barrier leads PhD candidates to get a severe case of writer's block leading to and resulting from much stress. Many dissertation advisors have a fear that their candidate will embarrass them in front of the other faculty and the field. Like artists who have trouble deciding if their painting or poem is good enough, dissertation advisors mull over whether their student is ready to get their dissertation approved. This leads to continuing revision.

Some PhD candidates complete the coursework and comprehensive examinations for the doctorate but never complete their dissertations. As a result, the landscape is littered with ABDs which stands for "All But Dissertation." Some ABDs will get jobs with lesser institutions if they feel or delude themselves that candidates will finish their dissertation before they start the job or shortly thereafter. Sometimes PhD candidates who obtain a job on the promise of finishing their degree don't finish it or spend most of their time trying to finish it, and therefore don't publish new research, which leads them to lose their job.

Evidence of this pressure on research is demonstrated by heavily subsidized PhD programs. Graduate students are given close to full tuition and paid a stipend that could be as much as $20K a year with the tuition at $40K. If we assume a minimum of three years, that is $160K. The argument in favor of this high subsidy is that graduate assistants are needed to help teach so the faculty can do more research. The Kingdom's faculty demand this subsidy and administrators yield to this demand for fear of losing their star research professors. The faculty considers the support for graduate students to be a key measure of the department's commitment to research. This means that the institutions who want to maintain their research brand have no choice but to spend hundreds of thousands, if not millions of dollars, a year for their candidates.

The training and testing of the scholarly quality of faculty does not stop with obtaining the PhD. New PhDs are like rookies in major league baseball. They could go to the minors, which in this case could be a community college, a think tank, less prestigious institutions, or some high schools that are firmly in the Kingdom. Or they could drop out of academia and make scholarship an avocation, living happily ever after.

The root cause of much of the individual and societal damage done by the Kingdom is the insularity created by the PhD training programs that leads to a culture where undergraduates are considered a burden. The culture has been called "monkish" by some colleagues. Monks are in monasteries where they communicate with each other. They have neither parishioners nor students. Their forte is not dealing with the outside world. The culture generated by PhD programs and reinforced by the publish or perish folkway needs to change. It is rare that a strong researcher who is a poor teacher is denied tenure or that an outstanding teacher with a modest research record is given tenure.

PhD training is where to start in improving undergraduate education to support the principles of equity and inclusion. The three traditional components of professors' duties, research, teaching, and service, must be given equal weight in the PhD course requirements. This would require less time and effort for content coursework, comprehensive examinations, and dissertations. It would require more time to be devoted to teaching and service to the department and the university that would possibly carry academic credit.

Public statements may give the impression of a less top-heavy research orientation, but the operating principle is to rate research higher than teaching and teaching higher than service. PhD students should take courses and have required activities on teaching, serving the department, the university, and the community. These activities should be structured and evaluated with the same rigor as research courses, comprehensive examinations, and dissertation work.

It may sound like these suggestions are like Don Quixote tilting at windmills, but it is already starting to happen as the Kingdom moves to maintain its tribes. Some programs are creating add-ons and a general realization by faculty of the importance of teaching and service.

As already mentioned, PhD candidates are encouraged and required to take teaching training seminars in recognition of the need to improve college teaching. The next step is to formalize these into apprentice training that generate credit courses required for the PhD. Bringing in an expert on teaching to hold a discussion or even several training sessions will not work because they are not the faculty to which the PhD candidates are beholden.

Requiring candidates to develop the skills and perspectives to be effective colleagues in the business of the department is also happening. Graduate students are demanding more participation in the formulation of department policies. Policies and procedures could be developed to ensure that graduate students are trained to do a good job as curriculum evaluators by participating in reviewing undergraduate student surveys in courses they work in as well as in graduate courses. Graduate students would have a more extensive role than undergraduates in their education since they have more and better experience.

In contrast, the professional schools may have a more open and flexible approach to the priority among the three components because they do not subscribe fully to the bait and switch business model. A professional school can ask their professor which of the three components they want to be most evaluated on for tenure or promotion. The Kingdom's faculty should be given the same option.

Finally, graduate students need to learn how to work for the university at large and the surrounding community of the university. Many graduate students join graduate student organizations which are sometimes unions. They practice being lobby groups pushing their own interests which is understandable and one approach to helping students act in the political process of the university. However, it is not enough if the purpose of the PhD is to prepare future faculty to be good citizens. For example, graduate students helping to improve undergraduate curriculum and courses would put them in the role of a citizen in the department working towards the public interest of the department. PhD programs that involve graduate students in the improvement of the undergraduate curriculum would prepare the graduate students to do the same when they become professors. Learning to be good citizens through PhD would create new faculty who work for the goals of their department even while they are pursuing their own self-interest.

If these suggestions are implemented in PhD training, there will be the added benefit of helping existing faculty take a less insular view of their responsibilities as faculty. Rather than put scholarly research as their main priority and the main priority of their department, they learn to be less insular and territorial in their attitudes and actions. They will see their graduate students as junior partners working for the good of the department, university, and community, so they will do the same.

NOTES

1. Britannica, The Editors of Encyclopaedia. "socialization." *Encyclopedia Britannica*, 16 Dec. 2022, https://www.britannica.com/science/socialization. Accessed 3 February 2023.

2. *5 Career Killing Mistakes PhDs Make (#4 Is Very Common) | LinkedIn*. https://www.linkedin.com/pulse/5-career-killing-mistakes-phds-make-4-very-common-hankel-ph-d-/. Accessed 28 Jan. 2023.

Chapter 20

Reform Lower Division Coursework

Do not confine your children to your own learning, for they were born in a different time.

—Hebrew Proverb

Too many faculty members teach like it is the 17th century. As noted in Chapter 6, The Student Prince Warning, the trinity of lectures, readings, and tests never worked from the beginning and works even less for 21st-century students. The trinity asks students to be human copy machines. When asked to find some information or come up with an idea, their ink runs out.

The trinity is particularly harmful in the first two years of college where most liberal arts and general education core courses are required. Dropout rates are highest, and so are student complaints, confusion, and anxiety. The students are forced into courses just like those they took in high school and to jump through hoops where high grades are the primary motivation. They are disappointed and confused because they thought college was going to be different from high school.

Elite students with strong academic backgrounds can weather the storm of introductory survey courses because they know and accept the drill or can avoid them by taking college credit in high school. Commoners face a string of survey courses which depend on lectures, readings, and tests which never worked for them in the first place. They may think the torture never ends.

The Kingdom's faculty too often assume that the purpose of these courses is to introduce students to their disciplines rather than help students develop a wide range of skills that will help them become professionals and adults or come to grips with how the world works and how they can find their place in it. The faculty think they have too much to cover to give the students a solid foundation in the discipline, so they think the trinity is the most effective and efficient way to educate students. Their dedication to the life of the mind and to the sanctity of their scholarly discipline lead them to teach the old fashion way.

Another factor contributing to the widespread use of the trinity in lower division undergraduate courses is the large class size. Once class size rises above 40, lectures instead of discussions and exercises are more likely, tests are easier to grade than papers, or they think big classes are too difficult to use project-based learning or group projects. Some faculty figure out ways to avoid the trinity, but most do not. How could the faculty know differently? The trinity is how they learned in college.

The predisposition toward the trinity is reinforced by evaluations of professors. When professors get bad reviews, low enrollments, or the Chair hears criticisms, the remedy of choice is a class visit to observe the lecture. The assumption is that students will learn from an entertaining or high academic content lecture. Lecturers, no matter how brilliant they are, have trouble competing with social media. An undergraduate who is a top student recently told me that she would rather listen to podcasts than professors about politics.

As noted earlier, the Liberal Arts Core under the Kingdom has become a buffet with an infinite number of combinations depending on whatever the student was able to cobble together. The students' courses may reflect their interests, but they are just as likely to be a result of whatever courses happen to fit students' schedules. Despite the never-ending faculty discussions over the categories, themes, and struggles within and between departments to define the core, students see the liberal arts requirements in the first two years as just a list of requirements with little rhyme or reason.

The idea that a coherent liberal arts core could be created by really good thinking demonstrates the life of the mind blinders of the faculty. The historical evolution of higher education from religious institutions and the limited amount of information in the Middle Ages led to the idea of the Renaissance Man, where it is conceivable that a given person would be knowledgeable in all fields. Today, it is not conceivable that any single person would be close to the Renaissance Man, so the three divisions of the Kingdom evolved. The Kingdom's political solution was to give equal attention to each of the three divisions. The liberal arts core was created out of political necessity, not intellectual coherence.

Courses offered in the liberal arts core are designed to introduce each of the various disciplines in the three sectors to students. As a result, the courses have no direct relevance to the students' interests. The goal of most lower division courses is to cover material. The faculty dutifully cover the material regardless of what the students learn.

"Introducing the discipline" for subsequent classes and recruiting students to that discipline is not what first- and second-year students need. It sends the confusing message that majors are really important when the general line of the Kingdom is that you will succeed in the goals of liberal arts no matter what major you choose. The goal of these introductory courses should help students develop what tools they need to succeed in college and after graduation and help them start to make sense of the real world and where they will fit in it. A secondary goal is to help students have a better idea of what they want to study in their third and fourth year and why, which rarely is connected to what careers they may want to pursue.

These goals cannot be achieved primarily through the trinity of reading, lectures and tests. Educational leaders and researchers have recognized this and pushed different forms of what is usually called "active learning." While there is some agreement even among some of the Kingdom's faculty members that active learning is a good thing, active learning is not a widespread practice in first- and second-year courses.

Active learning is a vague term that has little meaning other than students do something other than absorb and dispense information given to them. It ranges from discussions, simulations, role playing, flipped classrooms, inductive research activities, presentations, and even Kahoots. Modern technology has made it easier to incorporate active learning in classes, but active learning is not a new idea. It has existed from the beginning with the Socratic method, and continues with laboratories in the physical sciences, problem-solving exercises, and many other strategies. Active learning strategies tend to be used in upper division courses, and they are less likely to be used in lower division classes since the traditional goal is to create the groundwork for future scholarly work in upper division courses.

Active learning methods are much easier to design if the goal is to provide the skills necessary not just for college but life and to help students come to grips with the realities they will face. It would be a mistake to think that moving away from the trinity of lectures, reading and tests to a variety of forms of active learning is just putting old wine in new bottles. It will change the wine.

The most important and contentious content change is to reduce the amount of material covered in lower division classes. Active learning takes more class time which consequently leads to less content covered. It requires faculty to do some serious editing based on their priorities. Too many faculty think that more is better given their commitment to introducing the scholarly discipline.

Faculty try to cover as much content as possible, which means more formulas in Mathematics, more authors in English literature, more facts or concepts in Political Science, and more great scholars from the field. The disciplines themselves have so many subfields that not covering it all runs the risk of complaints from faculty whose subfields have not been covered. Faculty frequently use curves because they include so much on their tests, that few students can master all of the material as discussed in Chapter 10, "'Dumbing Down' is Dumb."

Reforming the lower division courses requires more practice of fewer concepts. It brings the concept of scaffolding to lower division classes. It conforms to the well-known principle of education that "less is more" or to the legendary quote of super bowl winning Vince Lombardi, "Keep it Simple Stupid."

Faculty also use curves as a way to teach to the top of class by having students compete with others on an individual basis and a way to discover potential recruits to the Kingdom. This is particularly true in the sciences and math as well as economics, where fixation on mathematical analysis is dominant. It does not make much sense for first- and second-year students if the goal is to help all students prepare for the real world.

Competition among groups of students in the class, however, can be a useful tool to help all students. Creating teams of students in large classes that compete with each other in coming up with answers to prompts is one form of active learning. A Political Science professor hoping to have students learn the impact of federalism on public policy, for example, may provide a definition and require students to pick the right definition in a multiple-choice test, which would not help students understand what impact federalism has on, for example, a social welfare policy. A classroom activity where groups of students tried to figure out which levels of government would be involved, for example, in the distribution of food stamps would more likely achieve the educational objective but take more time.

Abstractions can be covered more quickly in lectures and reading, but deeper and more inclusive student growth will occur with active learning. Elite students can more easily handle the abstractions than commoners because they have grown up with them and their brains are wired for abstractions. Exercises like the one described above would provide more accessibility for commoners than readings, lectures, and tests, but they would also interest elite students since they find it interesting to make applications.

Moreover, even students who can master abstractions easily have trouble applying ideas from one context to another. Hands-on learning requires more context that can serve as a basis for applying ideas to other contexts. The K–12 curriculum is an inch deep and a mile wide; the Kingdom's curriculum is still an inch deep but a thousand miles wide. At the lower division level, all of that material is like a blur to students.

Cutting down the amount covered raises the stress faculty have. If the amount to be learned is measured by how much stuff is covered, the faculty will think that using more time for active learning is dumbing down. However, if the goal of lower division courses is to master tools and figure out what the world is about and where students fit in, active learning is the opposite of dumbing down.

Competition for extra credit points among groups can become an engine for engagement by having groups, rather than individuals, earn the points. In listening to each other and collectively trying to figure out the best answer, students would be practicing the application of the concepts. Time on task practicing material is a much better way for students to develop their critical thinking skills. It will help them make more sense out of the relevance of the content to their view than if they crammed for an exam.

A final reason for the use of active learning in class is that the class time would be valuable, and students should be rewarded for attending class. Classes based on active learning would require attendance because the student is missing practice time. Classes where attendance is not necessary for high grades rely on the trinity, therefore, emphasize memorization and abstract reasoning. It rewards the better prepared students and provides no reward for the students who spend the time coming to class. Classes that incorporate active learning will increase student engagement and more critical thinking, and therefore, contribute to equity and inclusion. As a result, active learning requires attendance which must be part of the student's grade. Faculty who take attendance are more likely to know the names of students and increase the students' feelings of inclusion. Instructors may want to avoid taking attendance because of the time and energy required.

In a large class, active learning would require a change in the relationship between the professor, graduate assistants if there are any, and undergraduates. Faculty would have to create groups of students, ranging in size from three to eight, and undergraduate or graduate teaching assistants would have to manage and facilitate the groups. Faculty would talk less, and students would talk more to each other and to the faculty member about the contents of the course.

By participating in teams, students will learn to work together and increase their sense of control over their learning. This should help reduce the anxiety and fear of failure that accompanies learning new things. In a sense, they would have a support group to meet the challenges presented by the professor.

Over the past five decades, more of the Kingdom's faculty are using a wide range of active learning techniques as they search for ways to renew students' engagement. Resistance to the movement continues from the traditional faculty who think teaching is telling and are wedded to the notion that scholarship alone is the path to critical thinking and understanding. Those advocating active learning are hesitant to challenge the traditional liberal arts focus on scholarship and are constrained by that goal. However, they persist in spite of the risks because either they know it is the right thing to do or they are tired of bored and hostile students who fail to participate.

Active learning strategies also help students achieve the goals of Social Emotional Learning discussed earlier. Students will not see other students as individual competitors especially through group work. They may get caught up in their groups and see other groups as the "enemy," but they also have their own group as their supporters. These and other strategies are a way to help students improve their self-confidence with more intense personal relationships than usually happens in large classes.

Not all lower division courses need to give a large role to active learning, but many more could. Active learning in lower division courses will increase student satisfaction with their initial academic experiences in college and will increase student retention and smarter choices for their upper division coursework. Students will begin to see that experiential learning is powerful and a first step that leads to internships and better career exploration. They will connect their learning to the number one reason they came to college, to find a viable career path. While some courses could be based on readings, lectures, and tests in courses designed for first- and second-year students, the bulk of them need to embrace active learning strategies.

Chapter 21

Undergraduates As Responsible Citizens

The secret of education lies in respecting the pupil.

—Ralph Waldo Emerson

Undergraduates should become valued stakeholders who are listened to and participate in the design, implementation, and evaluation of their education. Stakeholders who have a structured and acceptable say in government make democracy what it is. The Kingdom needs to change its relationship with its undergraduates to build a better relationship between stakeholders and the Kingdom's policy makers.

Make no mistake, an enhanced role for undergraduates in the Kingdom is as threatening as the Declaration of Independence was to the Kingdom of England. It is about changing the power relationships between undergraduates and the faculty as well as the administration. Faculty and administrators may fear a breakdown in authority from such a transformation but continuing to prevent undergraduates from participation in the policy making and policy implementation is leading to lack of trust between faculty members and their students. The Kingdom's faculty members must gain the trust of undergraduates by sharing some decision-making and working with students as valued citizens. Just like a government needs its stakeholders to trust its leaders and share in some tasks of governance, the Kingdom needs to treat undergraduates the same way.

Paulo Freire in his book, *The Pedagogy of the Oppressed*, argued that the power relationship between the teacher and the student is dehumanizing and bad pedagogy. This viewpoint sees undergraduates as oppressed by their education systems. Students may not say they are oppressed, but their dismissive behavior, criticisms, and occasional protests suggest they are. Freire calls for students to take control of what the faculty do.

Paulo Freire was an academic sharing ideas with other academics that led to institutes around the world and many followers. His work may have helped support the current trend in the Kingdom to welcome experiential learning and more attention to undergraduates, but it did not start a revolution. It just created more research and scholarly exchanges. Not much else has come from his work because he sought a revolution that could never happen and, in extreme form, made no sense. Educated by the Kingdom, Freire generated some useful abstractions that created scholarship and discussion through various sub-tribes of the educational tribe.

The alternative to the revolutionary power change suggested by Freire and others is for undergraduates and the faculty to see themselves as partners in education. Specific actions described in the last two chapters and this one require that administrators and faculty members treat its undergraduates as citizens. Ultimately, equity and inclusiveness can only grow in the Kingdom as faculty and undergraduates learn to trust each other.

The modest steps in the right direction today are mostly built on intelligent faculty members attempting to get the attention and participation of undergraduate students and realizing that the traditional emphasis on scholarship has limited utility. It is happening because some faculty and some administrators want it to happen. The willingness to accept a power relationship that builds trust between the faculty and the undergraduates is necessary for those small steps to gain momentum.

The call for the enhanced influence of undergraduates in the governance of the Kingdom is not a call for revolution. It is a call for administrators and faculty to serve undergraduates better. For that to happen, the Kingdom needs to treat undergraduates as citizens rather than vassals. It requires building meaningful and ongoing relationships with those undergraduates who act responsibly and think about both their self-interest and the public interest of the Kingdom.

The undergraduates would benefit from an end of the bait and switch business model of the Kingdom but not an end to the Kingdom. They will still be served by much of the curriculum if faculty and administrators refocus some of the educational content from the life of the mind to life. They will want the value of liberal arts in allowing them to come into college with unclear career goals. The treatment of undergraduates as responsible citizens will build trust between undergraduates and the faculty and administrators of the Kingdom.

When it comes to power sharing between undergraduates and the faculty as well as administrators, the behavior of students has to change as does the behavior of faculty and administrators. The Kingdom's faculty has already demonstrated some flexibility in response to students. Some administrators are brokers between the undergraduates and the faculty and are ahead of most faculty in moving toward helping undergraduates achieve their goals for a college education.

The undergraduates have not shown the capacity to pressure for their needs in a way that leads to building institutional structures where undergraduates can voice their views in a constructive way. For the most part, most undergraduates have generally avoided actions to create academic change and acted like children who don't think their parents will listen. The result is passivity and occasional protests which rarely lead to sustained institution building.

The Kingdom's response to the idea of enhancing the role of undergraduates in design, delivery, and evaluation of their education should not be viewed through the slippery slope metaphor that if they give an inch, the undergraduates will take a mile. Although the Kingdom's faculty and administrators are territorial and prone to see everything as a negotiation with winners and losers, the original concepts of liberal arts and enlightened self-interest suggest a different kind of thinking.

Movement towards equity and inclusiveness requires the leadership of the Kingdom, both administrators and faculty, to do several things.

The first and most important action for the faculty and administrators is to treat students as responsible adults even though many undergraduates are not ready for that. A dean and a close colleague liked to say that the trouble with faculty is that they don't like teenagers. Adults who have come to college after some experience as well as teenagers coming straight from high school resent being treated like children. More faculty members may like teenagers if they were treated as adults.

The use of the term "pedagogy" to describe strategies of teaching is revealing since it originated from the Greeks and roughly means leader of children. Educators distinguish between pedagogy and andragogy, which is used to mean methods to teach adults. Educators don't make the distinction because they prefer to see learners as children who need to be led to knowledge. The assumptions about teaching students are different between those who use the methods of pedagogy and those who use the methods of andragogy.

The role of college for the vast majority of undergraduates is to provide a path to adulthood or if they are already adults to more professionalism, so why treat them as if they were children? The answer to that question is that the idea that undergraduates need to be treated as adults is scary and revolutionary to the faculty of the Kingdom. They think that would mean giving up control and authority over their students. The first rule of andragogy is that the interests of students must be considered in designing a course that challenges the bait and switch business model of the Kingdom.

Treating undergraduates as adults is key to the attitudes of both the undergraduates and the faculty. The undergraduates think they are adults anyways unless they severely lack confidence, so treating them as children does not help build trust with the faculty. They want to be treated as if they were adults. Faculty who see students as adults will provide a positive example of what an adult does. Students will have a powerful role model to follow.

The next most powerful way to improve the relationship with undergraduates is for the faculty and administrators to share information with students for making individual decisions and providing feedback on new curriculum ideas. One obvious practice that would help build student trust is for the university to provide the information to undergraduates so they can make decisions about courses and programs.

For starters, students should be able to review the syllabi for the next semester prior to registration for that semester. This idea may be common sense, but the task would be a big lift for faculty and administrators. Most faculty may not work on the syllabus prior to registration and changes in faculty at the last minute may result in different syllabi. It would require a higher priority than the faculty and the administration now have for helping students select courses.

Students should also know the grade distribution of the class the last time it was offered since degree of difficulty would answer one of the biggest questions students have about a course—how hard is it. Opposition to this would be widespread from most faculty members. Easy graders would fear criticism about grade inflation. Hard graders don't want to lose enrollment.

Transparency might also include the publication of student surveys on courses. One can imagine reasons why faculty would object. Not only would negative survey results impact enrollment, but it could also lead to no tenure, no promotion, and no raise. It could embarrass the faculty who receive poor evaluations. Without these kinds of transparent policies, students are forced to rely on Rate My Professor which tends to overemphasize extreme views and snarky but entertaining remarks by the respondents. If nothing else, it would teach undergraduates that the percentage of respondents is the most important question they should ask about any survey.

The call for transparency is closely related to another form of power sharing between undergraduates and the faculty–participation in course and curriculum design. Students are sometimes given a role in the process, but it is frequently informal where specific faculty discuss ideas with some selected students. This is a step in the right direction.

A more meaningful and powerful step would be if faculty asked undergraduates to advise them on course design and curriculum committees to have at least one non-voting student member. The student should be given some recognition, pay, or even academic credit for attending the meetings and doing tasks like getting the opinion of other students. Having students on a course or curriculum committee would help faculty think in an empirically based way about the impact of their decisions on students. It would counter the desire of most faculty and their committees from requiring too much assigned readings and dealing with content too much in the weeds to be accessible to students. Faculty would no longer have to conjure up their own ideas of what students would say.

Undergraduates should be based on curriculum committees as a non-voting member. Faculty would find it to be "too much" to allow undergraduates to have equal voting power to faculty. Undergraduates may not be competent to vote yes or no on a learning objective, but they are competent to present an argument to members of the faculty committee so its members can be better informed. The exchange will improve trust between the two.

When it comes to curriculum at the department or program level as well as at the liberal arts college level, the process for consulting with undergraduates is difficult but necessary. Faculty do consult with students informally, but these students are likely to be elite students who share the faculty's commitment to scholarship. Attempts at broader consulting like calling for a meeting of undergraduates are likely to turn up few students, the same kinds of students the faculty already consults, or commoners who are usually troublesome and lacking information.

The students may not be able to understand the politics behind the positions of faculty and the complexity of the decision-making process. Faculty might object to having undergraduates in their meetings because it would limit their free speech in saying such things as "let's word this in a way to increase enrollment." Despite the difficulties, the interests and views of undergraduates must be taken into account by the faculty members on the committee.

A more direct and powerful power sharing between faculty and undergraduates is increasing the use of undergraduates as teaching assistants in lower division courses. The practice is already widespread especially in the physical sciences and social science and could be used more in the humanities. The best approach to undergraduate teaching assistants (UTAs) would be for students who took the class the previous semester to become UTAs the next semester. The benefits for both the professor, the UTA, and the students in the class are significant. The UTAs would be a knowledge group who can use their experience to help professors improve the course. Particularly useful will be the advice on exam questions and prompts for written assignments. The professor could use UTAs to do things like take roll, answer specific questions from students, grade exams and papers, and coach the students.

The UTAs would help make large courses be more hands-on and personal. If graduate students are assigned to the class, they could assist in training and monitoring the UTAs, in course design, and class presentations which would not only help the professor, students and UTAs, but also prepare them to be outstanding professors as the Kingdom's education becomes more undergraduate friendly.

UTAs can be incentivized through payment or academic credit. They would become recruiters for the course or the program, and they would have experiences that would make them valuable in future curriculum and course design. They are becoming and will become more of a force for the fair treatment of undergraduates.

A final development that will serve to build trust between undergraduates and the faculty is the growing emphasis on experiential learning. Faculty who work with students as interns whether it be conducting research, being undergraduate teaching assistants, completing community-based projects, working for a client in an internship, or completing community service are joining the faculty in making their world and the community within and outside the university better. Students are not answering the professor's prompts but working out solutions required by the task and working together to produce a product or service. The faculty member is still the authority, however, students are no longer judged just by their performance according to the professor's opinion, but by the amount of time put into the effort and the degree to which mutual goals were achieved. The failure of a project does not mean an F. The quality and intensity of the effort is the measure of the learning outcome and should be graded as such.

These suggestions are concrete steps to break down the barriers between undergraduates and faculty. The steps will build a culture that does not now exist for most faculty and students in the Kingdom. Students will become responsible and valued citizens in the Kingdom.

A transformation in the power relationships between undergraduates and faculty will help to promote equity and inclusion. The voice of the commoners will create a better learning environment for all students and especially struggling students. High achieving students will help struggling students. When they work with faculty, they will represent the needs of the struggling students. The insularity of the faculty will diminish as the faculty and students trust each other and work together on the common goal of preparing undergraduates for life.

Epilogue

The Kingdom of Liberal Arts is already moving toward some of the suggestions in Part V as a result of pressures from students, their parents, and many of the influential players in society. Much more needs to be done to build on the Kingdom's progress over the past two decades.

A former college president of St. John Agresto, a traditional liberal arts college, opined in in the *Wall Street Journal* interview entitled "The Suicide of the Liberal Arts" that teaching of overly specialized disciplinary material is leading to the self-inflicted death of liberal arts.[1] Agresto would probably be in favor of the life of the mind as the primary purpose of an undergraduate education, but he would also want the life of the mind to speak to life rather than to immersing undergraduates into the jargon and theory of the many tribes and sub-tribes.

The biggest potential threat to the survival of the Kingdom is to change the name of Colleges of Arts and Sciences to College of Professional Studies and implement curriculum changes to serve the goals of most students. While the name change would increase enrollment, it would be viewed as the destruction of the Kingdom because it would be harder for faculty to act as if scholarship was career preparation. The name change would improve marketing to those students who are not ready to choose a specific professional school but do want the major academic purpose of their degree to be developing skills and exploring careers.

An experience with one of my students about 10 years ago, a refugee from a worn-torn country in Africa, raises the big question about the future of the Kingdom. I asked an associate dean if this student could avoid some of the requirements for the BA because of his talent and experience. My argument was that he had written a book published by a very credible publisher on his experience, and he founded a foundation that built a clinic in his country. The associate dean said there would be no wiggle room because if he wanted a liberal Arts BA, he needed to do what was necessary by the life of the mind. The student went on to write several books, raise and support a family, lead his foundation, was able to work with UN and nonprofit agencies, and become a leader of other refugees from his country. The student found the wiggle room and graduated with a four-year degree.

I understand and respect the associate dean's view to maintain the purity of the Kingdom's curriculum, but to avoid hypocrisy, he would need to support admissions standards that would only admit students committed to the life of the mind and capable of the level of abstract thinking implicit in a liberal arts education. If those academic standards were applied for admission as well as the grading of students in all courses, the Kingdom might avoid suicide, but it would become a rump program at the university, and small Liberal Arts colleges would disappear as some of them already are. If he chooses to continue the bait and switch system, he will not reduce the damage detailed throughout this book to undergraduates and to society. He will not create a new relationship between students and faculty. If the Kingdom makes these choices, how does the liberal arts degree lead to equity and inclusion?

NOTE

1. Riley, Naomi Schaefer. "Opinion | The 'Suicide' of the Liberal Arts." *Wall Street Journal*, 2 Dec. 2022. *www.wsj.com*, https://www.wsj.com/articles/the-suicide-of-the-liberal-arts-higher-education-students-teachers-educators-degree-america-learning-11669994410.

Index

AAC&U. *See* American Association of Colleges and Universities
ABD. *See* "All But Dissertation"
abstraction, 126; scholarship and, 81
abstract reasoning, 127
abstract thinking, 102
academic families, 31–32
academics, as term, 36
accessibility, of college, 106
accomplishment, anxiety and, 62
Acker, Kathy, 19
active learning, 125, 127, 128
admissions spending, 14
Advanced Placement (AP) courses, 12, 83, 108
advertising, 5, 58
Affordable Care Act, 90
African American students, 110
African American studies programs, 41
After the Ivory Tower Falls (Bunch), 111
The Aims of Education (Whitehead), 3
Alfred E. Neuman (fictional character), 58
Algebra 2, 105
Alger, Horatio, 12
"All But Dissertation" (ABD), 120
alternatives, to college, 15
altruism, 73–74
alumni, testimonials from, 7

American Association of Colleges and Universities (AAC&U), 9, 39
American College Health Association, 57
American Dream, 11–12, 83, 106
American Federation of Teachers, 80
American Philosophical Society, 21
American University (AU), xiii
andragogy, 131
anthropology, 58
anti-careerist pressures, 105
antipathy, to know-how, 4
anxiety, 57–64; of commoners, 59; of freshmen, 60; in high school, 57, 58; optionitis and, 60–61, 62; of teenagers, 58
AP. *See* Advanced Placement (AP) courses
APA citation systems, 107
approach/avoidance condition, 59, 62
aristocracy, 4, 28; medieval, xi–xii
Aristotle, 71
art, 85
Athenian Oath, 91
athletic programs, 105
AU. *See* American University
authority: educational, 35; professors and, 37

bait and switch model, 19, 46, 64, 106, 136; admissions spending and, 14; approach/avoidance experiments and, 59; College Board and, 12–13; college rankings and, 13; commitment to scholarship through, 40; Common Core and, 81; flawed evidence for, 7–10; K–12 education system and, 11–12, 79; machine, 11–15; military and, 14; scholarship and, 40, 44; weakening of, 54
Bart Simpson (fictional character), 58
best practice, 86
bias, liberal arts, 85
Blake, William, 7
Bloom, Alan, 42, 43
Boards of Trustees, 115
Born to Win, Schooled to Lose, 105
Bourdieu, Pierre, 45, 48
brand, knowledge as, 5
bucket lists, 63
Buddhism, xii
Bunch, Will, 111
business school, 63
business tracks, 11

calculus, 82
Campus Compact, 94
Canon, 42, 43
capitalism, 102
career confusion, 58
career development, 75
career exploration, 67
career preparation, 9, 46, 54, 68, 118
career services, xiii, 67–70
Carnegie, Dale, 23, 24, 25, 63, 90
Catholic Church, 40, 42, 44
celebrity testimonials, 7
chemistry, 21, 72, 105
Chinese students, 45
Chronicle of Higher Education, 19, 57
citation systems, 107
citizenship, 73, 111; education, 89–92; office of, 89; responsibilities of, 91–94, 129–35; skills, 89

City Council meetings, 90
Civil Rights Movement, 41
class division, 110
class size, large, 124
class warfare, 111
Clemenceau, Georges, 79
The Closing of the American Mind, 42
"co-curriculum" activities, 67
Coleman, David, 12
College Board, 12–13, 83
college completions, 106
"college for all," 11
College of the Arts and Sciences, SU, xiv, 23, 135
college preparation, 14
college public relations, 32
college rankings, 13
Columbia University, 24
commercial databases, 72
Common Core, 80–82
commoners, xi–xii, xiv, 31–32, 54–55, 57, 106, 109–12; abstractions for, 126; altruism by, 74; American Dream to, 83; anxiety of, 59; AP credit for, 12, 83; career services for, 69; college rankings and, 13; in community colleges, 107; experience credit for, 71–72; Franklin as, 20; harm to, 53; knowledge versus know-how for, 3–5; leadership roles for, 94–95; national scholarship awards and, 61; networks for, 62; PhDs and, 35; professional programs for, 15; professors and, 116; public education for, 79; self-help books for, 24; survey courses for, 123; testimonials for, 7; veteran students as, 14, 53
communication skills, 89–90
community college students, 107
community service, 73–74, 75, 94
competencies, 4, 5
competition, 126, 127
completions, college, 106
concurrent enrollment programs, 108

co-op programs, 75
Coplin, Bill, 19, 36, 89
courses: AP, 12, 83, 108; gifted, 84; one-credit, 68; remedial, 107; summer school, 108; survey, 123
Covey, Steven R., xi, 105
COVID-19 pandemic, 54, 57
critical thinkers, 100
cultural heritage, 33
culture: monkish, 121; war, 20

data analytic workers, 98
debt, 106
decision-makers, 98, 101
Declaration of Independence, 92–93, 129
de facto tracking, 84
degrees: health, 54; state high school requirements, 80; STEM, 54
DEI. *See* Diversity, Inclusion and Equity
democracy, 90
democratic participation, 93–94
Department of Education, 82
Department of State, 100, 101
Detweiler, Richard A., xi, 8
dissertations, PhD, 115
Diversity, Inclusion and Equity (DEI), 42–43, 64, 109, 110
doctoral candidates, 118
doctors, medical, 35
doers, thinkers versus, 97–103
dropout: rates of, 85, 123; stigma of, 106
dumbing down, 45–49, 126
Dunkin Donuts, 109

economics, 41
educational authority, 35
educational standards, 101
elementary schools, 84
elite students, 61, 123, 126
elitism, 45, 48, 83
Emerson, Ralph Waldo, 129
employment: rates of, 69; university, 74
English, 80, 105, 125

enrollment, decline in, 53–55
evaluation research, 86
The Evidence Liberal Arts Needs (Detweiler), 8
experience credit, 71–76
extra credit, 47

faculty, xii, 44; career services and, 70; citizenship education and, 92; experience credit and, 72–73; PhDs and, 38; power relationships with, 129–30; tenure-track, 31, 117
families, academic, 31–32
fear, 11, 58
federalism, 126
feedback, 92
female students, 54
financial crisis (2008), 54
Fischmann, Wendy, 8
food services, 74
Foreign Service, xiii
Franklin, Benjamin, 20–21, 23, 28
freedom, 99
free speech, 43, 133
Freire, Paulo, 129–30
freshmen: anxiety of, 60; equity for, 107

Gardner, Howard, 8, 47, 48
Garfield, James, 64
German model, xiii
GI Bill, xi, 14, 41
gifted courses, 84
globalism, 102
Goethe, Johann Wolfgang von, 97
good citizens, 91
GPAs, 60, 108
grade inflation, 46
graduate school, 63; rates, 69; students, 117–18, 121–22
graduation rates, 106; poor, 85
graduation speeches, 62
grassroots rebellion, 81
"The Great Faculty Disengagement," 57
greed, 11
Greeks, 131

guidance counselors, 14–15

Harvard University, 8, 36, 45
health degrees, 54
HEOP. *See* Higher Education Opportunity Program
hereditary factor, 31
heritage, cultural, 33
Hibben, John G., 23
Higher Education Opportunity Program (HEOP), 108
high school, 105–6, 123; admissions spending in, 14; anxiety in, 57, 58; AP credit in, 12, 83; business tracks in, 11; college rankings in, 13; counselors, 80; freshmen students and, 60; graduation speeches, 62; mathematics in, 82–84; sanctity of scholarship in, 54; science teachers, 72; state degree requirements, 80
history, 53
Hopkins, Mark, 64
Howard University, xiii
How to Stop Worrying and Start Living (Carnegie), 25
How to Win Friends and Influence People (Carnegie), 23
How You Can Help (Coplin), 89
humanities, 21, 40, 41, 43, 46, 53, 60, 102
HVAC, 107

IB. *See* International Baccalaureate (IB) movement
idealists, 89, 102
inflation, grade, 46
intelligence, 47–48
International Baccalaureate (IB) movement, 83, 107–8
International Baccalaureate Program, 12
internships, 5, 59, 76, 94, 100, 103; career services for, 67, 69; co-op programs and, 75; experience credit and, 72; growth of opportunities for, 68; promoting, 73

intrapersonal intelligence, 47
intra-university scholarships, 61
Iran, 40

James, William, 115
Job Core, 107
Johns Hopkins University, xiii, 45
Jordan, Michael, 7

Kierkegaard, Soren, 57
kinesthetic intelligence, 47
King, Larry, 89
knowledge versus know-how, 3–5, 21, 59
Kodachrome (Simon), 79
Kozol, Jonathan, 83
K–12 education system, 14–15; bait and switch model and, 11–12, 79; Common Core and, 80–82; equity and, 105–6; toxicity of, 79–87
K–12 teachers and administrators, 48, 72

language, English, 80, 105, 125
large class size, 124
Larry King Live, 89
law students, 97–98
learning: active, 125, 127, 128; SEL, 48, 64, 86, 112, 128
Lenin, Vladimir, 53
"Let's All be Gay Boys," 27
liberal arts education. *See specific topics*
Library Company of Philadelphia, 20
Lombardi, Vince, 126
"Lost in the Life of the Mind" (Coplin), 19
lower division coursework, 123–28
low tax states, 54
Luther, Martin, 41, 42, 44

Mad Magazine, 58
male students, 54
management, 103
marketing, 4, 62, 69; of community colleges, 107

market research, 101; tasks, 69
Marxism, 102
Massachusetts, 80
master's programs, professional, 118–19
mathematical intelligence, 47
mathematics, 47, 80, 82, 83–84, 125
Maxwell School of Citizenship and Public Affairs, xiv
MCAS, 80
Medicaid, 90
medical doctors, 35
Medicare, 90
medieval aristocracy, xi–xii
memorization, 127
mental health, 64
mentorship, 37–38, 117
merit-equity conflict, 111
messaging, 5
Microsoft Excel, 72, 84
Middle Ages, 124
military, United States, 14
Mills, John Stuart, 43
Mississippi, 81
MIT Press, xi
MLA citation systems, 107
monkish culture, 121
monks, 39, 121
muckraking, xiv
multiple intelligences, 47–48
music, 85
musical intelligence, 47
Musk, Elon, 27

Nabokov, Vladimir, 19–20
National Association of Scholars (NAS), 39
National Center for Education Statistics, 53
National Education Association, 80
national scholarship awards, 61
National Science Foundation, 117
Native Americans, 20
naturalist intelligence, 47
natural sciences, 40
nepotism, 31

networks, 62
newspaper publications, 118
Newsweek, 10
Newton, Isaac, 3, 43
New York State, 80, 81
95 Theses, 42
No Child Left Behind Act, 101
non-academic sources, 118
"not college material," 23
NYC Public Library system, 23

Occupy Wall Street, 102
office of citizenship, 89
one-credit courses, 68
online peer review journals, 118
optionitis, 60–61, 62
oral communication skills, 89–90

parochialism, 19
pedagogy, 131
The Pedagogy of the Oppressed (Freire), 129
peer review journals, online, 118
Pennsylvania Hospital, 21
people of color, 43
people skills, 73
petit bourgeoisie, 20
PhDs, 110, 118–22; commoners and, 35; dissertations for, 115; faculty and, 38; socialization and, 116–17
Philadelphia Contributionship, 21
physical sciences, 46–47
Plato, 23, 43, 119
police brutality, 43
policy: public, 90; social welfare, 126; studies, xiii; workforce, 79
political science, 125, 126
power relationships, 129–30
practice, 47
pre-med students, 97–98
preparation: career, 9, 46, 54, 68, 118; college, 14
"The Presidents' Declaration on the Civic Responsibility of Higher Education," 93

Princeton University, 23
printed journals, 118
problem-solving, 73
professional development, 112;
  skills, 62
professional master's programs, 118–19
professional schools, 4, 41, 58, 119
professional skills, 55, 67, 73, 74
professional undergraduate programs,
  xii, 4–5, 14, 15, 68
professor, as term, 36–37, 116
Protestants, 40
psychology, 24
public education, 79, 80
public policy, 90
public relations, college, 32, 101

quadratic equations, 82
quantitative analysis, 84; poor
  graduation rates in, 85

rankings, 7, 9; college, 13
RAs. *See* resident advisors
rat and cheese (analogy), 59
Rate My Professor, 132
rationality, 44
realists, 89, 102
The Real World of College (Fischmann
  and Gardner), 8
reasoning, abstract, 127
the Regents, 80
religion, 39–40
religious leaders, 39
remedial courses, 107
Renaissance Man, 124
research: evaluation, 86; market, 69,
  101; "research based," 9, 86; social
  science, 8; systematic, 7, 8–9
resident advisors (RAs), 74
responsibilities, of citizenship,
  91–94, 129–35
return on investment, 9
Rhodes Scholarship, 61
risk, 58
Robertson, Heather, 67

Rogers, Lindsey, 45
Romeo and Juliet (Shakespeare), 35

Sagan, Carl, 31
St John Agresto, 135
SATs, 12; tutoring for, 108
Saudi Arabia, 40
Savage Inequality (Kozol), 83
scholarship: abstraction and, 81; bait
  and switch model and, 40, 44;
  commitment to, 40, 67, 110, 119;
  decision-makers and, 98; devotion
  to, 80, 116; dumbing down and,
  46; focus on, 84, 111; of high
  school science teachers, 72; of
  mathematics, 82; mentorship and,
  37–38; monks and, 39; professors
  and, 36; rationality and, 44; sanctity
  of, 39, 42–43, 54, 59, 71, 73, 91,
  106, 108, 117; self-worth and, 116;
  undergraduate education and, 42, 43
scholarship awards, 61
School Board meetings, 90
School of International Service, AU, xiii
science. *See* natural science; physical
  science; political science;
  social science
SEL. *See* social emotional learning
self-help, 20, 24, 25
self-image, 4
self-interest, 74
self-reflection, 38
self-worth, 116
Shakespeare, William, 19, 35
Simon, Paul, 79
skills: citizenship, 89; communication,
  89–90; people, 73; professional, 55,
  67, 73, 74; time management, 73
*A Social Critique of the Judgement of
  Taste 1979* (Bourdieu), 45
social emotional learning (SEL), 48, 64,
  86, 112, 128
social intelligence, 47
socialism, 102
socialization, tribalism and, 115, 116–17

social justice, 42, 93
social media, 10, 41, 124
social sciences, 21, 28, 40, 41, 43, 46, 53, 60, 102; research, 8
Social Security, 90
social welfare policy, 126
social work students, 97
Socrates, 23
Socratic method, 125
spatial intelligence, 47
speaker series, 68
speeches, graduation, 62
standardized testing, 81–82
state high school degree requirements, 80
statistics, 80
Steinbeck, John, 11
STEM degrees, 54
stressors, 57
student activities, 74–75, 85, 94
student engagement, 127
student organizations, 94
The Student Prince, 27–28, 123
Study Abroad, 61
"A Stunning Level of Student Disconnection," 57
SU. *See* Syracuse University
"The Suicide of the Liberal Arts," 135
summer school courses, 108
survey courses, 123
Syracuse University (SU), xii, 54, 57, 72, 110; College of the Arts and Sciences, xiv, 23, 135
systematic research, 7, 8–9

teachers: high school science, 72; K–12, 48
teenagers: anxiety of, 58; vulnerability of, 84
tenure-track faculty, 31, 117
testimonials, from alumni, 7
testing: SATs, 12, 108; standardized, 81–82
theater, 85
thinkers, doers versus, 97–103

Thirty Years Religious Wars, 40
time management skills, 73
time-on-task, 47
Town Hall meetings, 90
training, 25
transparency, 132
tribalism, 41; socialization and, 115, 116–17
trigonometry, 82
Truman, Harry, 101
Truman Scholarship, 61
tuition costs, 105
two-year colleges, 107

undergraduates and undergraduate education: Canon and, 42; commoners and, 111; dumbing down of, 46; lower division coursework, 123–28; new programs for, 41; optionitis of, 60; PhDs and, 121–22; professional undergraduate programs, xii, 4–5, 14, 15, 68; as responsible citizens, 94, 129–35; scholarship and, 42, 43; self-help books for, 25; thinkers versus doers in, 97. *See also specific topics*
undergraduate teaching assistants (UTAs), 133
Union Fire Company, 20
United States military, 14
university employment, 74
University of Pennsylvania, 20
U.S. News and World Reports, xiii, 9, 13, 82
UTAs. *See* undergraduate teaching assistants

verbal intelligence, 47
veteran students, 54; as commoners, 14, 53
vocational education, 3, 15, 79, 82, 99
voting, 90
vulnerability, of teenagers, 84

Wall Street Journal, 135

"The War on College," 10
Washington, Denzel, 39
Washington University, xiii
Watt, Steve, 24
Wayne State University, xiv
Western religion, 40
Whitehead, Alfred North, 3
"Who Needs College," 10
Williams College, 64

women studies programs, 41
workforce: needs, 98; policies, 79
World War I, 79
World War II, 25, 111
writer's block, 120
writing programs, 4
written communication skills, 89–90

YMCA, 24

www.ingramcontent.com/pod-product-compliance
Lightning Source LLC
Chambersburg PA
CBHW030241170426

43202CB00007B/76